Remembering Concord

Remembering Concord

Articles from the *Look Back* Collection

Helen Arthur-Cornett

THE History PRESS

Published by The History Press
Charleston, SC 29403
www.historypress.com

Cover image: Concord City Hall c. 1905. *From the collection of Alec Patterson.*
First published 2005

Manufactured in the United States

ISBN 1.59629.080.3

Arthur-Cornett, Helen.
Remembering Concord / Helen Arthur-Cornett.
p. cm.
Includes index.
ISBN 1-59629-080-3 (alk. paper)
1. Concord (N.C.)--History--Anecdotes. 2. Concord (N.C.)--Social life and customs--Anecdotes. 3. Concord (N.C.)--Biography--Anecdotes. 4. Cabarrus County (N.C.)--History--Anecdotes. 5. Cabarrus County (N.C.)--Social life and customs--Anecdotes. 6. Cabarrus County (N.C.)--Biography--Anecdotes.
I. Title.
F264.C7A78 2005
975.6'72--dc22
2005015181

To *The Charlotte Observer*, its editors and staff.

Again, my thanks for turning me loose with a new and untried history column, "A Look Back," in 1988. Now I thank you, once more, for according me the rights to publish these columns in not just one, but more books on our local history.
I will always be grateful.
And again, my special thanks to Scott Verner, editor of *The Observer*'s publication, *Cabarrus Neighbors*. His keen editing and helpful suggestions have contributed greatly to any success "A Look Back" has achieved.

Contents

Preface

With upward of six hundred of my weekly "A Look Back" columns in *The Charlotte Observer*, it has been necessary to produce more than one book. Happily, this is the second compilation of these area history columns, now published by The History Press of Charleston, South Carolina.

While the format of the second book differs from the first one, the content of this new one will use material from the same source, my weekly "A Look Back" columns.

Here I must state, I am a newspaper reporter and columnist who loves history, so my columns, covering hundreds of topics from local history, are as accurate and authentic as I (and the editorial staffs of *The Charlotte Observer* and *Cabarrus Neighbors*) can possibly make them. If you find errors, please forgive. My hope is that you will find this book just as entertaining as it is informative about our unique history, which covers three centuries.

Again, thanks to all my fellow Cabarrus County and area citizens for your continuing interest in reading and learning about, and helping to preserve, the history of this special place—and for sharing your knowledge of it with "A Look Back."

Acknowledgements

Once more I will try to thank all of you who have contributed so much, in so many ways, to the success of my weekly "A Look Back" column for so many years. The list seems to grow ever longer.

Much appreciation to the Cabarrus Genealogy Society, its president Shelia Weaver and members Larry Hayer and Bernard "Bill" Cruse for asking to publish my columns in book form, and for all the support and assistance you have provided to produce it. To Larry Hayer and Bill Cruse, whose expertise and dedication made it all possible. Without considerable effort from all of you, these publications would not have come to pass.

My heartfelt gratitude to:

L.D. "Bub" Coltrane III and son Mike Coltrane of Concord Telephone Co. (today CTCommunications) and the late L.D. Coltrane Jr., founder and president of the company, history lover and publisher of *Progress Magazine*, for his employees and for area history lovers; to Judge Clarence Horton, historian, and Kathryn Bridges, former head of the history room at the Concord library, for their many years of exquisite local history research, which they generously shared with "A Look Back"; and to Alex Patterson, and his late "Aunt Janie" Patterson Wagoner, who compiled a massive collection of local history during her long lifetime.

Others who have shared with us: Guy Beaver Jr., Jim Ramseur, Ira Dayvault, Dr. Gary Freeze, Margaret Bost, Jane Harris Nierenberg, Edith Walker, Ada Rankin, Mary and Ray Cochran, Hank Utley, Tom Wingate, Janet Magaldi, W.E. Shinn, Ora Crooks,

Louise Linker, Bill Workman, Edith Arthur and her late husband Don, Ross Morrison Jr., Billie McAllister, Frances Long, Sam Boger, Irene Brown Price, J.M. Cooper, Carol Cooke and Bill MacRae.

Also, many thanks to the churches of Cabarrus County, especially those grand old mother churches of mid-1700 vintage—St. John's Lutheran, Rocky River Presbyterian, Poplar Tent Presbyterian, Bethpage Presbyterian and others. Without their early records, we would have little written history of this area.

Appreciation also for the Eastern Cabarrus Historical Society and its museum, The Concord Museum, and to the libraries of the county, and especially the history rooms in the Concord and Kannapolis branches. So many of our dedicated historians who have shared with us have passed on, but I'll try to name some of them: the irreplaceable Misses Addie and Eugenia Lore, John Sharpe Hartsell, "Miss Elma" Beaver, Morrison Caldwell, Rufus Barringer, Jack Foard, J.K. Rouse, Dr. J.E. Smoot, Lynn Trout, Ruth Cress, Robert Washington Allison, Billie Sapp Brown, Rosa Caldwell Foil, R. Ray "Radio" King, J. Lee Pharr, Max Durham and Sarah Walker.

I feel sure I have missed some who should be credited, but do forgive me, for I'm deeply grateful to all of you—past, present and future.

1950 letter takes us back to Lutheran Church School

Going through the stacks of papers on my desk one day, I came across some lovely, yellowed clippings regarding the "Old Lutheran Church School House." I think some of my ancestors—Caldwells, Wallaces, Barringers, Propsts among them—attended that little school back in the late 1800s.

I remember my father, the late Eugene Caldwell, saying it was in the vicinity of the old Clara Harris School on East Corban Avenue, now a part of Rowan-Cabarrus Community College. He may have gone there, too, around 1900, after several of his brothers and sisters learned their readin', writin' and 'rithmetic there.

Aunt Lole remembers

At any rate, an old letter, typed in 1950 and signed by Aunt Lole, was with the papers. I think it was written to the late Billie Sapp Brown, who was really good at keeping historical artifacts. With it, in fine old writing, was a list of students in that little school as of 1886. Here is what Aunt Lole wrote to Billie about the old school:

> *In regard to the old Lutheran Church school that your mother and I attended, I have written what I remembered of the school and how it looked to me. I forgot to say that it had been painted white, but it looked somewhat weather-beaten when we attended school there.*

I wonder if the old cemetery is still there? It was on the grounds. I remember that we had a croquet set there, and we played the game.

Surely that's the old Lutheran cemetery on the grounds of the old Clara Harris school building.

"I was anxious to see the old cemetery," Aunt Lole continued, "but we were in Concord such a little while that I had no chance."

Two-room schoolhouse

Here is Aunt Lole's description of the school:

There were only two rooms in the building, with cloakrooms in between the two rooms. There was little furniture in the rooms.

The desks were similar to what are used in schoolrooms today.

There was a wood heater in one corner, and we had to get water from a well, and we had a bucket with a dipper in it in another corner.

In another corner of the room one of the pupils sat alone, most of the time, because of broken rules. His name was Joe Smith; he was red-headed and freckle-faced.

After he had grown up I met him again, and we discussed his being punish[ed] most of the time. He said, "But all the kids liked me, didn't they?"

Just two teachers

The letter continued:

There were only two teachers: Miss Mollie Fetzer was the teacher of the primary grades, and Miss Winifred Pratt taught the more advanced pupils.

Miss Mollie seemed rather stern, but I found out she had a very pleasant disposition.

Miss Pratt was a wonderful teacher, so kind to everyone. She was my teacher and I loved her.

She had a little chapel organ that she played a hymn or two each morning.

I remember the first day she played "Onward Christian Soldiers" and it seemed that she often played that hymn.

Once I felt she was a bit unfair.

She said that she had given us one lesson, while each one of the class studied another. So we had to stay after school.

Hattie Mehaffey resented being kept after school, so she went to the cloak room, got her wraps and headed for the door. She had a sun bonnet on her head.

Miss Pratt called, "Where are you going, Hattie?" Hattie called back, "I'm going home."

She never came back to that school.

First taste of maple sugar

Aunt Lole told a few more stories about the school:

> *I remember Miss Pratt's home was in Erie, Pennsylvania, and some of her people sent her some maple sugar and she divided it with us. I thought it fine; as I had never tasted maple sugar before, and I still like it.*
>
> *We lived on Depot Street, and on our way to school we passed Mr. Bill Boyd's carriage shop, and he always spoke pleasantly to the children that passed.*
>
> *We also had to pass the jail, and one morning we saw a couple of sheets tied together and blowing in the wind from a second-story window.*
>
> *We found out that a man named John Winecoff, who was insane, had escaped from that window.*
>
> *He died shortly after that time.*
>
> *There was a boys school in this same building, a few years later, and I think Dr. Bikle was the principal.*
>
> *These are the pupils that I remember: Laura and Joe Goodman; Alida, Drayton and Harry White; Laura and Lena Leslie; Jennie, Effie and Vallie Brown; Emmett and Harry Swink; Lillie and Bob Wilkinson; David, Cecil and Brad Archibald; Fay and Chalmers Sims; and sisters Hattie and Slalie Castor.*

There were some other students whose names would be familiar to local folks—the Suthers, the Lippards, the Walters, Smiths, the Browns and the Calloways.

Aunt Lole added: "Miss Pratt married some widower in the Rocky River area. I think she left some children."

The reason I'm relatively certain Aunt Lole wrote to Billie Brown was because she put in this sentence: "I hope Rufus is in good health." And Rufus, of course, was Billie's husband of many years.

What a nice little peek into that era! I just wish we'd had a little more of Aunt Lole's memories about it all.

Old Concord *Standard*— And "Cousin Anna" likely said thanks, too

How Mary Anna Morrison Jackson, widow of General Stonewall Jackson, spent her Thanksgiving Day more than a hundred years ago, in 1888, must remain hidden in the ages, for the details of her life—though often well documented in area newspapers and family folders—just don't go that far. But we can tell you what some of her countless Cabarrus cousins were doing that day, many years ago.

The village of Concord had a couple of newspapers, including the *Standard*, which devoted a whole column to Thanksgiving. The day was being duly observed among the fervent Southerners hereabouts, even though it had been the Yankee president Abraham Lincoln who had officially proclaimed it a national day of thanksgiving twenty-five years earlier in 1863.

Incidentally, one wonders, historically, whether President Lincoln was uncommonly thankful in 1863 that Stonewall Jackson's death had removed his military genius from the ranks of the Confederacy, which seemed not to recover from his loss that year—and finally fell a year and a half later, thereby saving the Union.

By 1888, however, the South's difficult reconstruction was passing, and Cabarrus folk, at the end of another harvest season, officially expressed their day of thanks, perhaps with much of the rest of the nation. It is also likely that Cousin Anna Jackson, as she was widely and appropriately known, observed Thanksgiving Day in 1888, for she was raised most piously. And she lived just twenty miles away in Charlotte, an area closely related in character to Cabarrus County.

For Cabarrus, 1888 was a kind of new era. New textile mills were opening here.

Drama, electric lights, music, art abound

Prosperity and *growth* were household words. Culture—drama, music, art lessons, even a town band—abounded in Concord. The village had just gotten its first bank and its first savings and loan company. And, for heaven's sake, even the first electric lights had come to town, in a dazzling display at Captain Odell's mill at the top of North Union Street.

The *Standard* itself was new, launched January 14, 1888, by J.P. Cook and B.E. Harris, editors and proprietors. They were also principals at Concord Male Academy. (There also was a Concord Female Academy.)

That Thanksgiving week of 1888, our farmers were reaping the year's crops and terming the wheat harvest the best ever.

Concord's Colonel Paul Means, who had just been elected to the state senate, explained in the *Standard* why Democratic president Grover Cleveland had been defeated in the national election.

Thanksgiving origins discussed

The *Standard*'s editors discussed the origins of Thanksgiving, declaring, "Some say it was the legitimate outgrowth of a custom instituted by the Pilgrim fathers and is of an equal age with the colonization of New England" while others attributed it to a colonial Massachusetts governor and still others traced it to European harvest festivals. Cook and Harris philosophized, "You pay your money and you take your choice," but "there are no doubts as to the propriety of setting apart one day in which to express our gratitude to the Beneficent Ruler of the Universe...and don't forget the poor."

There was plenty to do here. *Peck's Bad Boy* was being performed at Caton Hall. The Firemen's Festival featured fun and a fortune-teller. Thanksgiving services were set at the Episcopal Church. The Methodist Church was crowded for the marriage of Charles Sherrill and Nannie Swain. And improvements were being made at the Club Room. (Where, I wonder.)

Usual bad news

Not all the news was good, however. A Blackwelder boy's illness proved fatal. Monroe Voils of Mount Pleasant was injured when scaffolding at his blacksmith shop fell in. George Hartsell died after falling from a fence. There was an ugly plague called the Itch.

Out at Harrisburg, the cotton market was lively and an Irish immigrant, Joe Baker, had just joined S.M. Stafford's firm as clerk. Said Baker: "Faith, this is a good country; a job for me on the third day." He wrote his brother to join him.

Alas, the *Standard* failed to describe a typical Thanksgiving dinner, but we can guess it would include the beef and poultry and ham the county had in abundance, and those many vegetables and fruits grown here. Of course there would also have been sweets the women would have concocted—much as many of us have each year on our day of thanks more than one hundred years later.

The *Standard* had some pointed suggestions that sound all too familiar today: Why not an anti–chewing gum club for girls, the editors wrote, and an anti-smoking club for boys? "These are awful habits," stated the editors.

Concord's nine hundred citizens made the most of New Year's Day 1889

For a quiet but growing village of maybe nine hundred mostly straitlaced souls, Concord was a-jumping on New Year's Day in 1889. Grown-ups and children dashed outside in midday with smoked glass they intended to use to watch an eclipse of some kind, but the sun, that "old god in the sky...got behind a cloud," lamented the *Standard*. As the town's newest newspaper, the *Standard* was preparing to observe its first anniversary on January 14.

The night before, New Year's Eve, as always, members of the county's military company had shot their muskets off as they paraded up and down the town's streets near midnight. ("It was meant to welcome in the new year, but it always scared me to death," recalled one of Concord's most senior of citizens, who was a small child in that era.)

Town drama lovers laughed through the Arthur Love Comedy Company's play *Senator Spreadeagle* at the W.C.J. Caton opera house and were ready for another—*Hoosier Doctor*. Concord's new string band was practicing with its newest musical instrument, a harp, "and a beautiful one, too," wrote the *Standard*'s editors and proprietors, B.E. Harris and J.P. Cook.

Fireworks explode magnificently

Townsfolk and their many out-of-town holiday guests were giggling about the latest escapade of Master Jimmy Young, young fireworks salesman supreme.

Seems he set up a makeshift stand in front of Mr. Walters's grocery store to sell those holiday noisemakers, but somehow a hot coal got in among the firecrackers and Roman candles piled there. Well, bystanders scattered and Master Jimmy dove for safety in a back alley while "a tremendous fusilade" of exploding, bursting fireworks flared and "swept the streets."

Villagers also told how Joe Cannon and George Murr singed their eyebrows while shooting firecrackers on New Year's Day. Injuries were minor, the *Standard* reported, "and will only interfere with their good looks for a while."

The brand-new St. Cloud Hotel was opening its doors this very New Year's Day on North Union Street, and many villagers planned to see it and perhaps dine in its restaurant.

There was also the small-town talk. Miss Annie Cannon was voted the sweetest girl at Peace Institute in Raleigh.

New Year's gunshots

And was there gunfire, a way out of town the previous night? "One or two shots were heard to reverberate almost from cloud to clay and from hill to dale," the *Standard* reported.

The Reverend E.A. Osborne came from Charlotte to conduct a New Year's midnight service at the new little Episcopal brick church on then–Depot Street. The village's committee for free schools had just arranged to have public classes taught in the town's private schools—Mrs. Cole's, Virginia Dare Institute, Concord Female Academy and Concord Male Academy.

That "little Harry Taylor, whose beautiful curls everybody noticed," died New Year's Day. And there were those inevitable New Year's hunting accidents, two of them fatal. ("The men always went hunting on New Year's Day," remembered our most senior of citizens. "It was always for quail. I think they mostly killed the quail all off.")

But in 1889, time and the business world moved on. Make a resolution, wrote the *Standard*, to patronize Concord businesses—including, of course, the *Standard* itself.

Village stores—Cannon and Fetzer and Yorke and Wadsworth among them—were planning their year-end inventories.

Total county tax intake: $7,000-plus

Cabarrus sheriff William Propst was beginning to haul in county taxes: $3,726 from the county's 220,477 one-eighth acres, $670 from the town's 487 lots, $246 from the county's 2,170 horses and $201 from its 1,628 mules, plus similar taxes and fees on marriage licenses, mercantile operations, the opera house, income and other properties.

Meanwhile, the county shelled out for such sundry items as $23.00 to build a bridge, wood to repair the public road, the hauling of coal to the jail house, $2.50 for J. Gilmer's wife's coffin and a goodly sum for work at the county poorhouse. County commissioners also paid J.W. Mehaffey $4.00 for ringing the courthouse bell.

Then the *Standard*'s editors had their New Year's say. "Wasn't Jan. 1, 1889 a beauty...? Have you made any good resolutions? Do you intend to keep them?"

"Modern" Concord compared with 1849

The editors compared 1889 Concord and 1849 Concord: In 1849, they wrote, most villagers lived in unmortgaged log cabins—unpainted, unplastered, uncarpeted and with few adornments—and they sat before "well-fed fires," burning on one side, freezing on the other.

They ate from a common dinner pot hanging in the fireplace beside the skillet and teakettle. They ate with a "back handle knife" and an iron or pewter spoon. Evenings were spent before a pitch knot fire, reading the weekly newspaper by a tallow dip candle. They told time by a sun mark on the porch. In the library were the Bible, an almanac and books about the three Rs.

But "no dyspepsia troubled them."

In modern 1889, the "contrast is clear," the editors wrote. White houses—plastered, furnished, carpeted—replaced the cabins and boasted fine chairs, handsome bedsteads with "Angel-sing-me-to-sleep" pillows, eight-day clocks, hanging lamps, wardrobes and dressing cases.

Of dining room and kitchen finery, the editors said, "There's no end, and bless you, the sweet tones of a Mason and Hamlin organ are heard in every neighborhood."

"What does it mean?" the editors asked. "What is that knocking so hard at many modern doors? What is that that tells of a burning pain which appears on so many faces?

"Verily this is an age of progress."

Harris and Cook had a last word of advice: "Beware of the New-Year-turn-over-a-new-leaf-fellow. He's done the same thing before." And then they signed off with the traditional closing: "A happy and prosperous year to every reader."

Concord's "Aunt Nann" whipped up hats of renown

Area folk today may be surprised to learn that Concord's "Aunt Nann" Lee Alexander created world-famous hats during the Gay Nineties, right in the town's downtown area. Oh, were her creations ever fancy, adorned with "flowers, laces, ribbons, fans, buckles, mourning veils, face veils, aigrettes, ostrich plumes and birds of paradise...and imitation butterflies." (Aigrettes, incidentally, are sprays of gems or bird feathers, such as those of the egret.)

Here I must thank my friend Billie Brown for providing an article written by the late Aunt Janie Patterson Wagoner in the 1960s describing Aunt Nann and that fabulous decade that was part of the Victorian age.

Flamboyant hats

Here I present what Aunt Janie wrote about Aunt Nann's flamboyant hats and her seven millinery shops—a business success that probably didn't come easy in those early years.

> *Since Confederate money was worthless after the close of the War Between the States and other monies were scarce for a considerable period that followed, and family funds were low, my aunt "Nann" Lee Alexander sought to enter a business career, although in that day and time it was not considered genteel for Southern ladies to work—outside of the teaching profession.*

> *It was while making hats and bonnets for members of the family that Aunt Nann discovered her talent and ventured to visit the work rooms and salons in the big cities of New York, Philadelphia and Baltimore to learn the art of millinery, and the business end of it.*
>
> *There she found a congenial atmosphere and created fetching hats in velvets, felts, straws, silks and satins.*

The article went on to explain Aunt Nann's early education: "'Miss Nann,' or 'Miss Nannie' first saw the light of day in Concord on Feb. 28, 1866 on the site of what is now the corner of Depot St. [Cabarrus Avenue] and Bell Ave. She was educated by private teachers, including Miss Lily Long; Mrs. K.L. [Columbia Eddins] Cravin, piano teacher; The Bassent Academy and The Chautauqua Summer School in New York."

Shops here and throughout North Carolina, South Carolina and Florida

"For many years, Auntie owned and operated an exclusive millinery store at 18 S. Union St., next door to Dr. Johnston's Drug Store; six other shops in Mooresville, Mt. Pleasant, Asheville, N.C.; Seneca and Easley, S.C., known as the Lilian Shober Hat Shop; and Clear Water, Fla.," the article continued.

In 1960, some of Aunt Nann's shop assistants were still living—Rose Harris, Mattie Lentz Blake, Julia McConnell and Lola Walter Lefler—but her complete roster also included Lida White, Della Sims, Dolly Plott, Mamie Pharr, Laura Brown Winecoff, Dora Stuart, Jessie Burkhead, Helen Patterson, Rose Young, Agnes White, Nancy Young, Mollie Brown, Maud Gibson, Mamie Gibson and Mary Galliger.

"Each season Auntie journeyed to the northern markets where she purchased hats and materials for her establishments." The bird feathers, of course, were used as adornments "before protective laws and enforcement put a stop to the killing and the selling of birds for the millinery trade."

"Season after season, fashionable and distinguished ladies came to her for their hats," wrote Aunt Janie. She continued:

> *Two invitations in ownership of the writer read as follows: "1891 Your Presence is Respectfully Solicited at the Opening Display Of Fall and Winter Millinery Sept. 15, 16, 17 and 18 at Miss Nannie Alexander's."*
>
> *A private mailing card, authorized by Act of Congress, May 19, 1895, "Arte Postale," postmarked Concord, N.C. March 1, 1912, is addressed to Miss Henrietta Dees, St. Charles Street.*
>
> *Portrayed on the reverse side is a lady wearing a bodice with a high collar, lace jabot and a tremendous rolled brim hat, with an arrangement of grape clusters with foliage, and an aigrette and the following invitation: "Opening Display of*

> *Pattern Hats and Novelties, To which you are cordially invited Tuesday night, March 21, 1912, The Rhodes Hats and Magnolia Ribbons, Very Truly Yours, Miss N. Alexander."*
>
> *One fabulous hat was a huge black velvet with a cluster of ostrich plumes poised high on the left side and light blue ribbon, patterned after the hat worn by Mrs. Sarah Kemble Siddons, English actress who posed for her famous portrait by Gainsborough.*

Her hat in portrait in national gallery

According to the article, "The portrait today is in the National Gallery, London."

Some of Auntie's hats were graceful leghorns from Italy—one enormous hat was trimmed in long black velvet ribbon streamers and a single red rose.

She never duplicated her models in exclusive dress hats.

Her prize-winning hats were modeled by charming ladies—ladies of quality, born to wear brocaded gowns and elegant hats.

So, just who were those women of quality? And where did those world-class awards for her elegant designs come from?

> *Early in Aunt Nann's career, they [the quality ladies who wore her hats] were Misses Helen Johnston and Mabel Means and later Misses Jenn Winslow Coltrane and Grace Patterson.*
>
> *Helen Johnston was tall and slender with a luxurious suite of blue-black hair, piled high on her regal head, with deep blue eyes and elongated neck while Mabel Means had light brown hair, expressive gray-blue eyes and bubbling wit.*
>
> *Jenn Coltrane's classical blonde beauty and intelligence were greatly admired and hers was an enviable record as National Historian General of Daughters of the American Revolution.*
>
> *Grace Patterson, who became Mrs. A.G. Odell, was considered very beautiful. She had chestnut brown hair and eyes and her tight little curls were like those of our mother, naturally curled.*
>
> *Her merry, rippling laughter was soft and musical and she was full of fun. She played the violin in the college orchestra, N.C.C.W.*
>
> *The article goes on:*
>
> *One of this writer's treasured possessions was a sheer, white horse-hair braided hat Aunt Nann designed and made for me as a young lady.*
>
> *The crown was encircled with an imported wreath of tiny pink sweetheart roses and dangling rosebuds, countless numbers of them.*
>
> *The dress worn with it invariably was a soft white China silk, trimmed in Valencennes lace.*

Prizes and diplomas

"Auntie captured numerous awards in the world of fashion which added luster to her name," Janie Wagoner wrote. "A 'designer of national reputation,' she achieved a notable distinction at the Pan-American Exposition in Buffalo, N.Y. in 1901 where she was awarded one of the grand prizes offered by the *Western Milliner*, [a] magazine devoted to the art of millinery."

She continued:

> *There were a thousand hats in the competition, representing every section of the country.*
>
> *Auntie received a diploma of honor for excellence of design, style and taste displayed in producing a trimmed hat of high merit, being a mid-summer dress-hat.*
>
> *Award was secured in open contest, Chicago, May 20, 1902, participated in by milliners everywhere.*
>
> *The contest was conducted by* Western Milliner. *Jenn Coltrane modeled the hat.*
>
> *On Feb. 12, 1915, Aunt Nann received a prize for an original design in a ribbon-trimmed hat in a contest conducted by American Authority of Millinery.*
>
> *She also received a diploma for millinery by the Mecklenburg Fair Assn.*
>
> *Aunt Nann designed hats for Henri Bendel, Fifth Avenue, N.Y. and for the Hamilton Millinery Co., Charlotte, one of the largest wholesale millinery houses in the South.*
>
> *She loved beauty in every form and she found joy in her long years of selfless service, especially at Eastertide.*

But of course, Auntie Nann, and any milliner, would have cherished the Easter season and the famed Easter parade. Wonder if those fabulous creations of old could have had a hand in starting the Easter parade?

And to think, today hats are almost passé—although seems I did hear recently that they may be making a comeback.

Long ago, lace and feathers went to the ball

More than a century ago, in 1892, a gala leap-year reception was held at the St. Cloud Hotel near Concord's square, near where the Hotel Concord stands today. Well, it must have been a stunner, for the old daily newspaper the *Standard* went all out, reporting not only which young ladies were escorted by which young gentlemen but also what elegant attire those Gay Nineties belles wore.

Diamonds, silk, ostrich feathers

There was Miss Ada Rogers (who would make quite a story herself), in white faille, *en traine*, with diamonds, who was escorted by Charles Wadsworth. Miss Annie Cannon arrived with a "Mr. Werrell," in her white henrietta, *en traine*, with angora fur. Miss Bell Bost, in black lace and forget-me-nots, entered on the arm of B.E. Harris.

Miss Lucy Richmond, in blue silk, was escorted by E.P. Mangum while Miss Nellie Fisher, in white swiss and flowers, was accompanied by Arthur Faggart. Miss Clara Oehler came with J.B. Harkey, dressed in black net with red ostrich feathers. Then there were the Cochran girls, Miss Minnie, in yellow silk and chiffon, escorted by Dr. Fitzgerald, and Miss Grace, in white silk, with John Yorke. One lucky belle, Miss Minnie Thompson, came in red silk with two escorts—Ed Hill and Joe Goodman.

There were others whose family names have remained familiar in the area for generations—the Misses Helen Johnson, Willie Richmond, Corinne Harris, Jeannette

Ervin, Mary Fetzer, Fannie Fisher, Lizzie Young, Maggie Neal, Jennie and Kate Smith and Lallah Hill.

Among the gentlemen were Q.E. Smith, Howard Cannon, R.L. Kesler, M.W. Ball, R.E. Ridenhour, J.C. Leslie, Rev. B.S. McKenzie, Will Morris and G.L. Patterson.

There were married couples and chaperones, too—Mrs. Dr. Archey (honest, that's the way they were addressed) in white silk and hyacinths, Mrs. Dr. Young in yellow silk and pearls, Mrs. W.R. Odell in black silk and diamonds, Rev. and Mrs. W.G. Campbell (she wore black net). Mrs. J.W. Cannon chose china silk and pearls while Mrs. R.E. Gibson came in black silk and diamonds. Two matrons (widows, perhaps?) were unescorted—Mrs. B.F. Rogers in black silk and Mrs. Anderson in gray cashmere.

The *Standard* article noted, "The entire assembly is indebted to Mrs. Dusenbury for her kindness and personal attention."

And they were related to…

The following is how historian Eugenia Lore some years ago identified many of those at the ball for an article in the late L.D. Coltrane's magazine *The Progress*.

Miss Ada lived in the house at Spring and Franklin Avenues now occupied by Tommy and Louise Craig. She married a Gorman, traveled extensively, adopted musical protégés. Miss Annie Cannon was daughter of David Cannon, a brother of J.W. Cannon, while Bell Bost was a sister of Mrs. J.W. Cannon. B.E. Harris was grandfather of Jane Harris Nierenberg, who today is active in area heritage circles.

Miss Lucy Richmond was sister to Maury Richmond of the Richmond-Flowe Company and an aunt of the late George Richmond of Concord Telephone Company. Her escort, E.P. Mangum, was superintendent of Concord Graded Schools. The Fetzer girls were daughters of Dr. N.D. Fetzer of Fetzer Drug Store, where Roberts Camera Store now sits. Miss Oehler lived in the Poplar Tent area.

Miss Fisher lived in the castlelike Josiah Fisher house that once stood at Union Street and Grove Avenue. Arthur Faggart was a popular Concordian, father of Preston Faggart. John Yorke, a brother of A. Jones Yorke, married Miss Ada's sister, Miss Fan Rogers.

Jennie, Kate and Quint E. Smith were children of Sandy Smith, who lived in the big house beside Central Methodist Church that became the YMCA and later the community center and library. Quint was a civil engineer and Concord's city engineer for many years. Corinne Harris, who married J.F. Shinn, was the mother of Annette Shinn. R.L. Kesler taught public school music and was organist at First Presbyterian and Central Methodist Churches.

Jeannette Ervin married J.F. Hurley, editor of the *Concord Tribune* and later the *Salisbury Evening Post*. Fannie Fisher married R.E. Ridenhour, owner of Bob's Laundry. J.C. Leslie was an uncle of bank president Tom Ross. Gowan Dusenberry was prominent in social circles and best known for manufacturing Gowan's Pneumonia Cure.

Even an Episcopal priest

The Reverend McKenzie was an Episcopal minister whose name appeared in the diary of Miss Emma Atkinson. Will Morris was a prominent landowner. G.W. Patterson became postmaster. R.S. Wheeler was superintendent of Kerr Bleachery.

The Reverend Campbell was minister at St. James Lutheran Church. Ed Hill was brother of Miss Lallah Hill. Their father owned Hill's Tin Shop. Joe Goodman became owner of Gibson Drugs. The Odells were grandparents of the late John K.P. Odell.

What a nice nostalgic look back at an old hotel, long gone, and an era also long gone. Descendants of many of these early Concordians still live here a century later.

"Dummy" rail line ran briefly over Concord streets

About noon on March 10, 1892, "Railroad men saw a queer-looking object come blowing into the west-side train yard and switch to a side track at the Mecklenburg Iron Works." It was "the celebrated dummy engine that pulls the passenger and freight cars for Concord's Street Railway," revealed an article from the old *Charlotte News*, reprinted in an 1892 issue of the *Concord Daily Standard* and finally reported in a 1978 copy of *Progress Magazine*. The Concord Railway Company launched the little engine on its routes over certain streets, but in March 1889, it had been limping badly, the news story continued.

Jaunty little engine limping

"The *News* heard of the arrival of this distinguished visitor and hurried down to greet it. We found that it was in trouble and had come over here to be doctored by Capt. Wilkes," the article explained.

A crank pin had been broken off in a wheel, and it was found necessary to run the dummy over to Charlotte to have the broken pin drilled out and a new one put in.

> *Mr. W. M. Smith, one of the owners of the Concord Railway, was in the cab with the engineer. The engine made the trip over the Richmond and Danville line, working "on one side," that is, the driving rod on one side was relied upon to bring the engine here.*

> *The trip was made in about 35 minutes. The dummy consumed only about 50 pounds of coal between Concord and Charlotte.*
>
> *The repairs will be completed this afternoon, and by the time the* News *gets there, the people of Concord will hear the familiar rumble of the dummy along their streets.*

Well, the editor of the *Concord Daily Standard* begged to disagree! In a paragraph at the end of the *News* story, he added, a day or two later: "The dummy has not yet returned....Friend Harris is slightly in error about the time required to get to Charlotte. The engine was not allowed to run on a faster schedule than 10 miles an hour." This is a compelling addition to our lore on the short-lived dummy line.

Lasted a few short years

The railway company kept the dummy engine running for just a few short years. Sometimes the passengers had to get out and help push the engine up hilly or rain-wet local streets.

The article was researched by Concord's late historian Dr. J.E. Smoot, who pored over the minutes from many early Concord council meetings to get it. Smoot's research began with an entry on a town council meeting dated February 25, 1889, which was "To consider and confirm a mutual contract between the city of Concord and the promoters of a Concord Railway Company to haul both freight and passengers between the Southern Railway [depot] and the city of Concord."

Streetcar led to first macadamizing

The railway company may have spurred on the first paving—"macadamizing"—of several city streets, including Union Street North. On October 8, 1889, at a regular meeting, the council ordered the street committee to confer with the company about grading and paving streets "adjacent the Odell Manufacturing store," at the corner of Church and Buffalo Streets. (Many old-timers in the late twentieth century remembered the quaint little shop that once stood on the corner beside the old Locke Cotton Mill.)

On November 12, 1889, there were some complaints about the railway company's grading, and fourteen days later, at a called meeting, company president J.P. Allison "expressed willingness to exercise all reasonable care in the [grading] difficulties." In fact, Allison assured the street committee "they would grade and macadamize the street at Odell's store."

The city seemed favorable to the spirit of the project, for on December 10, 1889, the council "appointed P. B. Fetzer to borrow $100.00 from the Concord National Bank to pave North Union from the Methodist Church to the bank corner at Depot [now Cabarrus Avenue] and Union Street, on both sides of the Concord Railway Company's tracks." Imagine today, paving a street for one hundred dollars!

An editor's note outlined the engine's route: From the depot, east on Corban Avenue to Spring Street; then, because the train couldn't make a right-angle turn at Union and Corban, it made "a sweeping curve" from Spring to Union Street North. Then it ran up Union Street, across the square, almost to Marsh Avenue, where it turned east at the ARP Church, onto Church Street and then to Locke Mill. Many may remember that children made a playhouse of an old passenger car left on a siding built on Marsh Avenue.

Stop the streetcar whistle?

There's more: At a meeting on July 13, 1891, "The mayor was requested to ask the President of the Concord Railway Company to have the engine whistling stopped" while running over city streets. At a meeting on August 31, 1891, it was ordered that no freight or passenger cars could be pulled, but must be pushed, over any railway tracks in the city—except from Corban to Union at the town hall. And last, at that same meeting, the council decreed that "no dummy or railway engine shall be run at speeds greater than 7 miles per hour through any street except Corban."

Little train chugged noisily over city streets

That little-train-that-could chugged for some years, over and around city streets during the exotic Victorian era. More on the street came from a nifty short article published in 1949 while all of Cabarrus County was celebrating—vigorously and colorfully, I might add—the 150th anniversary of the discovery of gold here.

Lavish 150th birthday celebration

The celebration involved a whole week of beauty pageants, concerts, barbecues, hog-calling contests and a special edition on history during that rousing observance in 1949. The *Concord Daily Tribune* produced a special Gold Sesquicentennial edition, literally crammed with a wealth of Cabarrus County history. The article had no byline, but I'd bet hard cash it was written either by the late Mary Frix Kidd, for many years a fixture at the *Tribune* and an ardent and conscientious historian, or the late Ray "Radio" King, editor and also a lover of local history.

I wish they'd written a lot more about our town as it was in the 1890s...

> *One frequently hears the question, What would our great-grandparents think if they could come back to Earth and see the changes that time has brought?*
>
> *Equally thought-provoking is this question: What would you see if, like Mark Twain's Connecticut Yankee in King Arthur's Court, you could turn back the clock of time to the Gay Nineties and look at Concord's Main Street?*

Deep mud sidewalks, public well

Here's how the article answered the question:

> *You'd see a straggling street, not too wide, considerably muddy and sidewalks so deep in mud that a Gay Nineties Sir Walter could have a chance to demonstrate his gallantry after every rain.*
>
> *You'd see the public well in front of what is now Kale-Lawing's store* [in 1949, on the corner of Union and Corban], *horses tied to the hitching posts along the street or drinking from the watering trough;*
>
> *Women wearing trailing dresses with waspish waists, bustles and sleeves so wide two women could scarcely pass each other without the necessity of dirty looks.*
>
> *Probably the most interesting sight would be a little train laboring noisily up the middle of the Main Drag.*
>
> *This was the famous "dummy," used by many, discussed by nearly everybody, and probably "cussed" by a few, because of its frequent habit of getting off the track or stalling as it rounded what is now the Corban-Union corner.*

Little engine ran from depot

The term *dummy* refers to the undersized steam-powered locomotive used to draw the small train. "Because the business section and the Odell Mill were so far from the depot, William Smith, J.P. Allison and others formed a company and built the dummy line, which began at the depot, ran up West Corban street to the [former] site of Morrison Lumber Company.

"There it forked to the left, a spur tract ran behind the stores behind Hoover's and Lore's store," which later was Efird's, in the area where Roberts Camera Store is now.

"To the right, the line ran to the Corban-Union corner, [which then was] the square, turned north and proceeded up Union Street to about the location of the L.H. Sides Home," near Marsh Street, I believe.

"There it made a sharp right turn...and ran up Church Street to the rear of what is now Locke Mill" and today is Locke Mill Plaza.

Passenger car added

The article continued:

> *At first, the little engine, puffing and belching smoke, drew only a freight car in which goods brought in over the Richmond and Danville Railroad could be*

> *brought up town to merchants and the products of Concord's cotton mills could be carried back to the depot.*
>
> *Early in January 1891, Editor J.P. Cook mentioned in the Daily Standard that a passenger car had been added and was frequently used by "drummers"* [salesmen] *coming in* [on trains] *to work the Concord trade and stop at the St. Cloud Hotel.*
>
> *By that time, the dummy had been in use long enough for its engine to need frequent repairs, and once it was put on the Richmond and Danville tracks and driven to Charlotte for a thorough overhauling.*

Horses often ran away

According to the article, "Horses frequently became frightened at the noise of the dummy and ran away. In August, 1891, Editor Cook wrote, 'two horses hitched to a hack took fright at the dummy and ran down main street, and under the awning of St. Cloud Hotel.'

"Engineer W.H. Elliott drove the dummy at that time."

Some of the *Standard*'s files between 1892 and 1904 are missing, so what happened to the little dummy train—not a true streetcar—apparently is lost in time, the article noted. Later editions make no mention of it. It is believed, however, that it ran here about five years, perhaps to the mid-1890s.

Old tracks make WWII weapons?

Old-timers today can recall those old tracks running on the town's main streets and how passing cars would slip and bump a bit driving over them. There's a rumor that the tracks were ripped up and sent to the federal government to be used in the World War II effort, but I couldn't verify this.

There are so many other unanswered questions: Did the little dummy run on a regular schedule, based mainly on railroad train arrivals? Could passengers wave a hand and stop it to get on? And what was the fare, if any? When it bounced off the tracks, how was it put back on, and who put it back? Was it ever pulled by real horsepower? Who were the engineers?

Undoubtedly it was steam-powered, because there was no electric power. But what was the fuel—coal or wood? Did it make money, did it lose money, or was it started as a nonprofit venture to benefit merchants and mill operations? And when that little dummy reached the end of its line, so to speak, what became of it? Perhaps we'll never know.

Play ball, Concord: 1897 cranky rooters stir excitement

Here's a glimpse of the riotously comic Concord–Mountain Island pennant game of 1897. Those rabid Concord rooters, adorned with red and blue ribbons, were, it was written, "the most intense set of cranks ever gathered in a grand stand."

This information comes from well-known local baseball fanatic Hank Utley, who found a nifty news account from the time of the dramatic 1897 Concord–Mountain Island pennant game. (Mountain Island, incidentally, is on the line between Mecklenburg and Gaston Counties.) "It was not known that the rivalry between the two clubs, or feeling, was so high," the article began, "until the arrival of the teams and their contingents."

Rabid fans in bright colors

The article went on:

> *The Concord Special brought in 125 Concordites. They came in as they went out, with flying colors.*
>
> *Hats, canes, umbrellas, coats and dresses were ornamented with red and blue ribbon.*
>
> *Every Concord man or woman represented 100 pounds of enthusiasm to the square inch.*
>
> *The intensity of feeling was not confined to the players or rooters but to the ladies and older citizens who came along as part of the most intense set of cranks ever gathered in a grand stand.*
>
> *Concord had the town. It was her day, and Charlotte gladly welcomed her.*

The keys to the city were turned over to the visitors by Mayor Springs and they were assured of full liberty to do whatever they would: holler as loud as they would and, in fact, claim the town for the day.

Betting heavy in hotel lobby

"The lobby of the Central Hotel was headquarters for the rooters. There and on the sidewalk in front of the hotel much backing of judgment was done," continued the article.

> *The bets were 5 to 3 on the Concord team by the Concord men. Mountain Island's representatives, though few, were game. They bet the Concord men to a standstill in several instances.*
>
> *The town was agog with excitement.*
>
> *Concord chose the right of the grandstand; Mountain Island rooters took the left.*

Excitement beyond measure

The reporter went on to describe the mounting tension:

> *There have been sights and scenes galore in that grandstand before, but there has never been any excitement surpassing or equalling* [sic] *that of yesterday.*
>
> *Concord had her "yellow kid"* [Hinton Willeford] *and other almost equally ardent rooters; Mountain Island had some backers who were equal to these star members.*
>
> *The clash of their wit and smart talk kept the grandstand in a continuous uproar.*
>
> *Confident of an easy victory, Concord's star aggregation was dismayed beyond words when the Mountain Islanders scored thrice in the first inning.*
>
> *Concord was struck dumb with astonishment. The local outfit went scoreless in both the first and second stanzas only to see Mountain Island increase their lead to six runs by pushing over another trip in the third.*
>
> *Misenheimer made things a little more cheerful in Concord's half of the third by making the first hit and scoring the first run off the delivery of Parker, Mountain Island ace.*

Things look bad for Concord

The outcome of the game seemed uncertain:

> *Mountain Island scored her seventh run in the fourth and things looked worse than ever for the Cabarrus lads.*

> *Bill Weddington, Concord's star twirler, was taken out of the box with* [a] *temperature of 101 in the fourth and Mangum and Bailey, University of North Carolina battery, were sent in.*
>
> *Taking heart, the locals pushed across four runs in the fifth only to have the Gaston boys send their eighth counter over in the sixth, making the score 8 to 5 in favor of Mountain Island.*
>
> *Through stellar stickwork of Bailey, Reed, Misenheimer and Brumley, Concord scored four runs in her half of the seventh and led, 9 to 8, until their opponents pushed over a counter in the ninth to knot the score.*

Tremendous effort gives Concord win

The article had a happy ending: "In the first of the ninth they [Mountain Island] scored another, but, undaunted, Concord pushed two across to win the game 11 to 10." What a finish, Concord!

And who were the Cabarrus men and women—red ribbons even flying from their parasols—who went to that big game? You may recognize a lot of the names: the Youngs, Yorkes, Rogerses, Lowes, Crowells, Gibsons, Hills, Ervins, Wadsworths, Pattersons, Smiths, Wagoners, Kluttzes, Goodmans, Whites, Ballards, Lentzes, Bosts, Barriers, Browns, Caldwells, Hoovers, Richmonds, Boyds, Drys, Cobles, Urys, Kings, Montgomerys, Pitts, Floyds and Doves.

The article's official postmortem:

> *The University battery did good work for Concord. Concord's fielding was clever. She had very much the best of her opponents in this line.*
>
> *Misenheimer played well. The catchers of both teams did magnificent work.*
>
> *Both teams deserved victory for they fought nobly.*

In the 1930s, such local greats as Ulmont Baker, Bobby Hipps and Bill Steinecke turned Webb Field into baseball miniwars on many a hot summer night.

Baseball becomes society game

In those years, baseball in Concord rose up to become a society game. Affluent families bought front-row box seats and invited lucky friends to sit with them. Ladies of Concord's Junior Charity League daintily threw in the first baseball as each season opened.

Those games usually produced a fight or so, especially when Kannapolis was out there with Concord's Weavers. The field fisticuffs were sometimes eclipsed by the startling explosions of bursting lightbulbs when the cool night air hit the hot bulbs in that primitive lighting system around Webb Field.

A Depression note: There were always little boys who stood outside waiting to catch foul balls, not to get inside the stadium, but to add to their slim store of playing equipment. You see, the Depression-poor town could afford little for recreation in those days. Ah, yes, folks. Good old days, good old times, despite the hard economic conditions.

Civic clubs went all out for 1928 game

Those "crank" Concord baseball fanatics who, in 1897, shook up Mecklenburg County, rootin' for their hometown team, didn't have a thing on the Concord Rotary and Kiwanis fans of 1928.

A reporter at the *Concord Daily Tribune*, who had a nifty sense of humor, wrote the advance publicity and the account of the comic 1928 battle of the bats fought between the Concord Rotarians and Concord Kiwanians. It had to compare with the legendary Keystone Kops.

They came from New York?

This game was, the report claimed, the "Season's Classic," and so important that even New Yorkers headed south to see it. Read on:

> *One-eyed Connally, gate crasher de luxe, was last seen surreptitiously boarding a Southbound train in Pennsylvania Station, New York City.*
>
> *When questioned regarding his hasty departure, he replied: "I haven't missed crashing an important athletic event in more than 20 years and I shan't start now. Haven't you heard of the baseball classic of Cabarrus County that will be staged in Concord Thursday afternoon between the Rotary and Kiwanis clubs of that city?"*
>
> *His interrogator was awarded a look of withering scorn when he admitted that he hadn't.*
>
> *Forewarned is forearmed, but if Gate Keepers F. C. Niblock, Rotarian, and Gilbert Hendrix, Kiwanian, can keep the elusive single-lamped genius from sifting through without paying the nominal two-bit fare they will become the envy of every professional ticket-taker in the land.*
>
> *Tex Rickard will gladly reward either, or both, with a permanent berth at the turnstiles of Madison Square Garden for their vigilance.*
>
> *Connally should reach town today if he is successful in running the gauntlet of passenger car conductors that obstruct his way South. Otherwise, he will probably hit the city on a freight just before game time Thursday.*
>
> *His presence will add color to the occasion, if not money in the treasury.*

Winner to play Life Insurance Underwriters?

The reporter continued:

> *The winner of the contest has been challenged by the Life Insurance Underwriters of the city for a title contest to be played on a selected date within the next few weeks.*
>
> *Because of their victory last year over the lawyers they feel that they should at least be considered as possible holders of the urban gonfalon.*
>
> *Victors of the civic club struggle will act on the challenge early next week.*
>
> *No date for the chicken barbecue that must be given the winners by the losers has been set but dusky hirelings of members of each club have mysteriously been relieved of daylight work to make up the sleep lost during alleged nightly excursions.*
>
> *Fouls and fowls will help make this classic one of the most to-be-remembered baseball games in sporting annals of the city.*
>
> *Leon Godown has unanimously been chosen chief arbiter by members of the two baseball committees.*
>
> *He will call 'em as he sees 'em and take sass from no man.*
>
> *Players who attempt to give free advertising to spectacle manufacturers may find themselves ousted from the game and fined for their incorrigibility.*
>
> *With muscles loosened again after a single practice afternoon, the Rotary Club will match the Kiwanis line-up* [with the following]*: Glenn Hawfield, first base; Dick Rankin, second base; Kay Patterson, third base; Bill Bingham, short stop; Bob Ridenhour Jr., Lee Miller and Bill Brown or Pat Ritchie, outfielders; Bill Morris, catcher and Rob Bell, pitcher.*
>
> *In addition to his duties around the hot corner, Kay Patterson will be relief hurler extraordinary.*
>
> *Utility players include Parks Lafferty, Bob Jones, Phil Sherbondy and Wayne Blanks.*
>
> *Harvey Moore will be the master mind on the board of strategy of the rotating papas.*
>
> *Gus Hartsell is said to have been busy for the past week borrowing thermos bottles to provide liquid nourishment for the benefit of those affected by the heat or the excitement of the conflict.*
>
> *Everything is set for the biggest afternoon of the year. Push your worries aside for several hours and join the Big Parade toward the Webb Field portals.*
>
> *And don't become inspired by the deeds of One-Eyed Connally as, to emulate his mischievous.*

It is unknown who the Kiwanians who faced the awesome Rotary nine were. Their coach was the late great Manley Llewellyn, well-known Cabarrus lawyer who once pitched for the New York Yankees.

And who won that epic battle of the civic club bats?

1928 baseball game scored laughs

Well, Concord's public-spirited civic club men didn't produce a Mighty Casey at the bat on that spring day in 1928, when baseball mania reached a peak hereabouts. But the Concord Rotarians and Kiwanians did make the trek to the field May 25, prepared to battle to the end for a plate of chicken barbecue. Here's what happened during that "game of the century," as it was reported in the *Concord Daily Tribune* of May 26, 1928:

> *Committing a travesty on baseball, Kiwanians and Rotarians went through seven innings of agony and laughter for the sake of a chicken barbecue at Webb Field Thursday afternoon.*
>
> *And when the Bureau of Weight and Measures rendered its tragic report, the score was 9 to 5 in favor of the Kiwanians and their appetites.*
>
> *The big lame-back and muscle-bound fracas elicited from the cash and free customers more laffs than laughing gas.*
>
> *There was much to be tickled over with such illustrious clowns as Dr. Joe Pike, Albert Palmer, Lee Miller and Manley Llewellyn performing.*

First circus outside of a tent

The article went on:

> *The crowd admitted it was the first circus it had ever seen assembled outside of a tent.*
>
> *Dr. Joe Pike resembles the trademark of a Michelin tire after his bouncing program. Swarthed in bandages and smelling strong of hoss' liniment, the only thing that can be recognized about Dr. Pike today is his bald head.*
>
> *He is appearing incognito on the streets because he couldn't run bases for Fred Shepherd. He fell down and bounced about in true rubber ball fashion.*
>
> *Albert Palmer proved beyond a reasonable doubt that when it comes to the monkey business, he knew his peanuts.*
>
> *This stellar* [excuse the adjective] *second-sacker could catch balls rolling his way in times of leisure, but when spheres bounded down his way in other intervals they rolled to the outfield.*
>
> *Judge Palmer demonstrated the art of base-running very hilariously. He moved off the bag, fell down but couldn't get back in time to be safe.*

Digging into the serious side, if it can be located, the game was more or less a duel between Llewellyn and Bob Bell, the latter hurling for the Rotary team.

Llewellyn struck out sixteen men and allowed four hits.

Bob Bell was less effective. His wildness offset his strikeouts. He whiffed eleven men, but allowed six free bases to first. . . .

The Kiwanians outshined the future dinner hosts in base-running. The whole Kiwanis outfit had taking ways, swiping eight bases.

Dr. Ed Misenheimer hooked half of the eight besides catching a real nifty game. The latter also rapped out a nice two bagger.

Not more than six balls were hit to the outfield. The out-fielders passed away the time by playing immediately behind the infielders or day dreaming in the grassy spots on the outer rim of the park.

Many hits were obtained by poking the sphere lightly into the infield.

Magic? The comedy continues

The reporter went on with his colorful commentary:

There was quite a bit of magic unfolded for the fans to solve.

Both Bell and Llewellyn struck out nine men each in the first three innings, giving up two or three hits in the meanwhile, but the scoring nevertheless was heavy.

The catchers either dropped the ball on the third strike or the batter was walked. Once on base, it was easy for anyone to score.

The infielders and outfielders simply couldn't find the handles on the ball by which to hold them.

Dick Rankin, Rotary second-sacker, had an awful time of it. He couldn't catch, hit or run.

His next door neighbor, S.G. Hawfield, had about the same luck down at first base.

Kay Patterson at the other side of Dr. Rankin caught up with his afternoon sleep.

The Rotary outfielders were often invited to come as far as the infield and watch the game.

They did, never endangering the chances of victory.

The Kiwanis outfield enjoys ballgames too. It marched into the infield to enjoy the fun. Dr. D.G. Caldwell, Mayor C.H. Barrier and Fred Youngblood were the Kiwanis outfielders.

The infield support [for] *Lindy Llewellyn consisted of Ray McEachern,* [first] *base and star of the struggle; Judge Palmer, second; Eb White, shortstop de luxe (didn't catch a ball) and Fred Shepherd, third base (he caught two balls and threw one almost a mile high over Ray McEachern's head).*

Umpire Godown took no sass

"Leon Godown as umpire took no sass," proclaimed the article.

There's a bit more in the "stats": Rotarians Miller, Bingham and Bell got a total of four hits, and Kiwanians Caldwell, White, Palmer, Misenheimer and McEachern got a total of six hits. "Pike ran bases for Shepherd in fifth and fell down trying to do it."

So much for a riveting game of 1928 baseball. But don't they sound like good old days in many ways? You reckon it was fun? Most everybody knew most everybody. Town leaders and civic clubs good-humoredly squared off and apparently had a lot of fun along with the sore muscles and aching backs. And in 1928, the daily newspaper could print caustically funny accounts of their antics—and not have to print retractions, corrections or even apologies.

Stroll down Union Street, see much of our past

Many folks enjoy walking, jogging and running over Concord streets. Most any day, on a drive down Union Street, from Buffalo Avenue down as far as the sidewalks go south of the city, you'll see joggers out in flocks. As they dutifully trot along, they see big homes and big trees that arch into shady green caverns. They whiz through a downtown that is being increasingly restored toward a two-century-old past—with old-style lights reminiscent of gaslights, cobbled sidewalks and some restored old business buildings, all to attract ever more business prosperity to the historic downtown.

Union Street—long known as Concord's main drag—has retained some features from its past. The towering old trees, for example, have long been a source of city pride. Some of those imposing old homes have survived the march of progress as well, although too many have fallen to the wrecking ball. So for many, it's reassuring that the business district, which became drastically modernized in post–World War II years, today is gradually changing back toward its heritage look.

In an article by an unknown author, there's a glance at what walkers of two or three generations ago saw as they strode—usually not by choice—on Union Street to shop, to go to work, to meet friends or just to while away those slower times. The article appeared in *Progress Magazine*, the late Lester Coltrane's telephone company publication, which featured much local history. The unknown author really knew the people and places of Concord. Much of the article's information is credited to David Suther, a coffin maker, and to shoemaker David Murr, also a deputy sheriff from 1874 to 1876. Both are old Cabarrus names. David had to be related to the late Inkie Murr, a Concord police chief in the middle years of the twentieth century.

A hotel, a tailor, a church

The author begins with Dr. John Fink's store in the old wooden American Hotel, which sat on the same site as today's Hotel Concord. Just north was tailor Bob Price's home, which was where the old Cabarrus Theatre showed its Hollywood films, especially during World War II and afterward. That's where the administrative offices of First Charter National Bank are today. Central United Methodist Church remains on its old site, but with a new building today.

A bit north was the home of an important Cabarrus figure, Caleb Phifer, who helped get Cabarrus cut off from Mecklenburg County in 1792. His home was removed for First Presbyterian Church to build its impressive building. Just beyond the church is Charles A. Cannon's white mansion, built on land once occupied by the widow Spears and her two sons, James and Pea. On northward a way, Union Street forked—one branch to Salisbury, the other to Beatties Ford Road.

North Union was extended northward to Buffalo Avenue, years after the Concord Cotton Factory was built in 1839. Today it is Locke Mill Plaza, a restored condominium complex. At the top of Union, at Buffalo Avenue, is Wheatfield, the white mansion Captain J.M. Odell built in the late 1800s. The iron grillwork fence still surrounds it.

Suther brothers' blocks

On Union Street south from Cabarrus Avenue (formerly Depot Street), the Suther brothers, Rineholdt and David, owned the east side of Union Street for a block or two. Their home later became the site of the Cannon and Fetzer store, which still later housed parts of the old Belk building. Today that site is a mall-type operation with a sports bar, furniture, jewelry and gift shops, offices and a bakery and deli.

Caton's Bar (A bar? In Concord's downtown?) sat on the corner of Union and Depot Streets, where a clothing store operates today. Then came Sam Kestler's buggy shop, beside the alley, and three Phifer and Yorke "storerooms."

A Confederate commissary here

"During the Confederate War, the building [beside the storerooms] that was later J.F. Dayvault's Meat Market...was used as a Confederate Army commissary supply station," the author wrote. "This section of North Carolina, in fact most of our beloved southland, was greatly impoverished and almost destitute during and following the Confederate War."

The article continues: "All able-bodied men were called into military service and hardship became the order of the day....Daily sacrifice was a necessity," and the Confederacy set up commissaries to aid families of soldiers who needed help. Concord's commissary, in the meat market, opened July 17, 1861, and assisted nineteen families in its first fifteen days.

Below the commissary was Kiah Harris's "brick row," and the Kluttz home, on what today is the site of the 1876 Cabarrus Courthouse. Below it, to Corban (which the author spelled "Corbin"), were Joel Reed's drugstore and R.W. Allison's General Store. Past Corban Avenue was Burton Groner's house and little store, where the *Concord Daily Tribune* operated for years. Beyond were R.A. Brown's two-story brick home, the Stowes' rock house and Mrs. Quantz's home.

Washington Lane was just a private entrance to Alfred Brown's home and backyard tanyard. It was continued for years by his son George. Then came Charles Blume's Wagon Shops, "built under the great oaks that today adorn the spacious lawn of the Charles F. Ritchie home," well beyond the town's limits and about where the little village ended.

Union Street joggers see city's rich historic past

On our nostalgic jog along Concord's Union Street—once described as "the sweetest and greenest in the South" by the august Tarheel Josephus Daniels—I'll point out the sites of some long-gone establishments such as the town's early academy and a Ku Klux Klan lodge. Those intrepid joggers who cover city miles in snow, heat, cold, whatever should realize how little this two-century-old town's main drag has changed since the 1800s. Happily, much of Union Street's historic look seems to be surviving, despite efforts to modernize it after World War II.

Today, some of the imposing old houses are gone, including a castlelike one in stone, near the downtown. That devilish Hurricane Hugo took a terrible toll on many of the street's gorgeous towering trees.

Past the jail and shops

We'll now start at the square and go south on the west side, where Roberts Camera Store is today. That's where the 1839 jail sat, beside the town whipping post, stocks and pillory. Next was David Bostian's home and tailor shop. Bachelor Archibald "Baldy" Moss's store was next, followed by George Stephen Murr's place, where City Hall sits today. Then came Dan Stiller's little house beside an alley, which was later closed.

Beside that was Colonel Daniel Coleman's property, where the city utilities department is now. It also used to hold "the home of the misses Mahan...who conducted a very select boarding house." From there almost to the corner of Union and Corban was Dr. Kiah Harris's property, which held his Harris Hotel—now a row of vacant buildings owned by Cabarrus County, across from the new and historic courthouses—and Harris's large livery stable.

Near the middle of Corban Avenue, flanked by St. James Lutheran Church and a service station, was the county's two-story brick courthouse, which boasted a belfry. The courtroom, on the second story, was reached by a winding, outside staircase. There also was "a public well of the finest water in the world," according to David Murr. County offices were on the first floor. Destroyed by fire in 1875, the courthouse was promptly rebuilt across Union Street—today's restored Historic Cabarrus Courthouse.

A plank road toward Fayetteville

West Corban Avenue then was a plank road that led to the depot, after the railroad came to town. Eastward, the plank road led toward Fayetteville, passing Barrier's old mill, beyond Cold Springs Church. South of Corban was John Phifer's house, which later was owned by Robert Foard, father of our feisty young Confederate soldier Fred Foard. Fred was captured by Yankees, leaped from a speeding train on his way to prison and roamed the Pennsylvania countryside, matching wits with and eluding enemy patrols for weeks.

Robert Foard operated a large store and a hotel, which today is the site of the St. James Lutheran Church parking lot. It's still sometimes called the Foard Corner. Colonel John Osborne Wallace (my great-grandfather, incidentally, who was Cabarrus clerk of Superior Court) owned the land from Corban to Windy Lane. From there to Chestnut Street the land was owned by Rosie Kluttz and later by William Blume, who built the two-story brick home still called the Blume House.

Town limits extended

The original town limits later were extended from the Wallace property to Chestnut Street.

Now, traveling Union Street to the north: The Confederacy's Victor Barringer and General Rufus Barringer owned a long stretch between Cabarrus Avenue and Fisher's Lane (today, Grove Street), along with Dr. L.S. Bingham and J.S. Fisher. Northward was the A.M. Brown lot, some James Black property, and the "quaintly beautiful" home of wealthy, respected merchant Robert "Wash" Allison—he of the black cape and hat. The Cannon house on that same property was formerly occupied by Cabarrus Academy.

Next came the Smart and Allison homes, on land owned by blacksmith Philip Brown.

Of churches and the Klan

In the late 1860s, the Central Methodist Church parsonage was on the corner of Mill Street (Franklin Avenue today) and Union Street—and that meant the residents could get water from Russell Spring, or Big Spring, which gushed mightily on what today is Coltrane-Webb school property. John Rogers (the oldest Cabarrus surname) lived on the Franklin Avenue corner and owned frontage up to Marsh Street. Samuel Sloop's home and "splendid wood shop" were on the southwest corner of Union and Marsh.

Two Lutheran ministers—Heilig and D. Dreher—owned land adjacent to the old Archibald home beyond Marsh Street. The Ku Klux Klan lodge was on the rear of the adjoining Irwin property. Then came the Little John Long house.

The early Concord Academy was behind the next lot. Academy Street was named for it, but not until it was opened in the 1870s. Next came the home of Thomas Eagle, bricklayer and watchman at McDonald Cotton Mills. The W.R. Odell house later was built on that site.

Thus was prestigious Union Street, perhaps 100 to 150 years ago. So runners, enjoy what you know now of your lovely exercise route.

Buffalo Bill and Annie Oakley shot many thrills into Concord

Buffalo Bill was "a fine figure of a man," wrote a local old-timer who saw, in person, that nigh-world-famous man who came to Concord with his boisterous Buffalo Bill's Wild West Show around 1901. With him was that nigh-world-famous markswoman Annie Oakley, who showed local folk her extraordinary skills in person. The old-timer, unfortunately, was not identified in the article written by the late local historian Rosa Caldwell Sides Foil, who recalled for us those early days when circuses, fairs and carnivals were really big deals in Cabarrus County. Her recollections were printed in the 1970s in a fall issue of L.D. Coltrane's *Progress Magazine*, published by Concord Telephone Company. Here's how those memories went.

Wild West Show camped on barbecue site

"About 1901, Buffalo Bill's Wild West Show came to Concord and erected its tents on the Charles McDonald property which was across North Church Street from the Cabarrus Creamery."

"What's unusual about this?" the article asked about the event. "Only that Buffalo Bill himself was with the show and with him was Annie Oakley, the U.S. Markswoman." Buffalo Bill was William Frederick Cody. He was born in 1845 and became a Pony Express rider and a government scout and guide.

Cody also contracted with the Kansas-Pacific Railroad "to provide meat for the laborers, and in 18 months [1867–68] killed more than 4,000 buffaloes." Buffalo Bill also "engaged in numerous Indian fights; organized his highly successful 'Wild West Show' in 1883. He died Jan. 17, 1917."

The old-timer, in his article, inserted a glimpse of local importance: A local woman, "Mrs. Charlie Griffin, the daughter of the Reverend J.P. Hipps, is distantly related to 'Buffalo Bill.' Her grandmother was a Cody, a cousin of the famous plainsman." The old gentleman also wrote a bit about Oakley, whose full name was Phoebe Anne Oakley Mozee.

Annie shot well from horseback

This remarkable woman "demonstrated her skill with her Winchester even when riding a horse at breakneck speed—so expert that she outlined the profile of an Indian in headdress on the target board," according to the article. "The lines of bullet holes were so accurate that it appeared as an artist's drawing."

The writer, "then a small boy," remembered Buffalo Bill as "tall, erect, [wearing a] cowboy hat, deerskin jacket, white mustache and goatee." He continued:

> *The show was a thrill no boy could forget. Real honest-to-goodness cowboys and Indians. It was a cowboy and Indian performance and they really put on a show.*
>
> *The cowboys could rope and bulldog a steer in "nothing-flat." Their skill with the lariat was something to behold.*
>
> *As one of their stunts, they would choose some unsuspecting young couple and lasso them, pulling them close together—much to their embarrassment.*
>
> *Several covered wagons, forming a wagon train guarded by a formidable group of heavily armed cowboys, entered the arena.*
>
> *They drove around the ring several times and then formed a tight circle in the center, as though camping for the night—a campfire was lighted in the center—then all fury broke loose.*
>
> *The wild, blood-curdling yells of the Indians as they rode out—full speed—to attack the wagon trains. Rifles and revolvers spat fire, smoke and noise, as the Indians rode in a circle, bareback and on fast Indian ponies—pandemonium reigned.*
>
> *To make it more realistic, one wagon always burned.*
>
> *Suddenly it was over—you could almost feel the quiet—the only sound was your own heart thumping in excitement as you felt the top of your head to make sure you still had your scalp.*

I really would like to have had a little more of that early gentleman's memories of that momentous event in the life of quiet little Concord in 1901. He told it well.

A dog and pony show

Now here's the same man's account of Gentry Brothers Dog and Pony Show, which was charming but not quite as heart-stopping:

> *The heart of every boy, girl and many adults thrilled each year when the posters announcing the coming of the Dog and Pony Show were displayed.*
>
> *Each year, the tent would be erected on the "Wagoner lot" on Depot Street, about where the Carol-May Hosiery Mill now stands.*
>
> *It was a gala day and entire families would attend together. The show had no attraction other than highly trained small animals.*
>
> *There were dozens of beautiful, well-trained ponies, many of them handled by boys and girls. The various tricks they performed were beyond belief.*
>
> *And dogs galore. Never before or since has the writer seen such perfectly trained animals.*
>
> *Then, too, there were the seals, and we marveled at their dexterity and sense of balance.*
>
> *And monkeys and clowns aplenty, much to the delight of the audience.*
>
> *Of course there were lions, tigers and other wild animals in cages, but never a wild animal act.*
>
> *This was just a good, clean family show and they never failed to show to a packed tent.*

This is how it was for Concord and Cabarrus County, in the good old days. There was so much about those times that was good—and always enchanting for us to learn about today.

Way back when, this was City Hall

On the downtown Concord corner where City Hall sits—oops, the City Hall Annex today—once stood a fortress-like brick building with a tower and an opera house. It, too, served Concord as a city hall, for more than half a century. It was stern, impressive and ornate with fancy brickwork. Out of its big white double doors would dash the town's spirited matched gray fire horses when the fire bell sounded.

Beside the city hall, to the right, was an old building that still is in use today, in a remodeled state. There was an empty lot beside it that today houses the Morris building (the area where Your Gym fitness center is and where J.C. Penney Company used to be).

Sadly, that handsome old city hall was demolished in the 1950s to make room for the new city hall, which the city again outgrew, so it's now the City Hall Annex.

Behind the city hall, was the old First Presbyterian Church, a plain little brick structure built in the 1803s.

Historic First Presbyterian demolished

That historic little church, which sat atop the old First Presbyterian Church graveyard, was demolished sometime around World War II to make room for a grocery store and parking lot. Few pictures remain of it. In the late 1800s, South

Spring Street had not been cut and paved, and there was no wall around that beautiful Memorial Garden—the restored and beautified First Presbyterian Church cemetery.

Today's city hall building is farther north on Union Street in the old Citizens Bank/ Pastime Picture Show buildings. Thanks to an article in the late L.D. Coltrane Jr.'s *Progress Magazine*, we can read a bit of the old building's history.

The old city hall: A showplace

That city hall, in 1902, wrote an unidentified historian, "added much to the attractiveness of our downtown section; indeed, one of the show places of Concord.... It was ultra-modern, three stories high and provided much needed facilities for city and civic needs. Our citizenry could hardly wait to tour the new building." As the article suggested, let's take an imaginary tour alongside those early Concordians. Here is what they might have found:

> *As we approached the granite steps at the building entrance we may have been greeted by a beloved police officer, Mr. R.C. "Bob" Benfield, who would have graciously conducted us through the building.* [Mr. Benfield served our city well for many years.]
>
> *We walked down the hall, passing the stairway on our left, and arrived at the first office.* [There weren't any offices on the right.]
>
> *This was the police station and the office of the Chief of Police. All law violators were brought here following arrest.*

Potbellied stove: Chewers' target

The article described some interesting features of the old building:

> *A small potbellied stove sat on a bed of sand in the middle of the room. The sand was held in place by a frame of 2 × 4's nailed to the floor. The purpose of the sand was to keep hot coals off the floor.*
>
> *However, it also was the target for some "hit a dime at 20 feet" tobacco chewing citizens.*
>
> *The north and east walls were lined with split-bottom chairs. Cuspidors, or spittoons, were strategically placed in the room and in the southwest corner was a large oak roll-top desk.*
>
> *Here, resplendent in his blue uniform, sat Chief of Police J.L. Boger. He was a man of strong convictions, believed in law enforcement and served our city well.*

A much-used opera house

Too bad that that massive, ornate city hall is no more. It was so impressive, it seemed to hold its own with the imposing county courthouse (now the Historic Cabarrus Courthouse), almost directly across Union Street South. Let's continue our tour of that haughty old municipal fortress and opera house.

> *Next we were shown the office of His Honor, The Mayor, J.B. Caldwell (my grandfather, incidentally), who had succeeded Mayor M.B. Stickley.*
>
> *Continuing down the hall, we found two additional rooms occupied by the city Tax Collector, Mr. Ross McConnell.*
>
> *The four offices were inter-connected and were lighted with sixteen candle power, carbon filament, electric globes.*
>
> *Further down the hall we arrived at stairs leading to a somewhat damp and musty basement area which housed the city jail, or calaboose.*
>
> *The several cells were very securely enclosed with iron bars, heavy metal doors and massive locks.*

The "tour" then "returned to the first floor and up a stairway to the second floor":

> *In front of us, on the north side, were two offices. We turned left, in the spacious hall, and entered through a double door into the new "Opera House."*
>
> *There was a wide aisle in the center paralleled by two lesser ones on the sides. We continued down the rather steeply ramped center aisle, between rows of wooden theatre seats, to the elevated stage.*
>
> *In front of the stage was the orchestra pit. . . .*
>
> *Many one or two night engagements were booked, featuring Shakespearean plays, minstrels and vaudeville.*
>
> *Home talent plays were frequent and many public meetings were held. These programs brought much enjoyment and entertainment to our community. People came from miles around to see the shows and attend the meetings.*

Fire horses ready to go

The article also described the early fire department:

> *On the ground floor behind the large white doors which opened on the sidewalk was the fire department.*
>
> *In the middle of the room, near the front, two sets of harness were hung, suspended by ropes from the ceiling. The collars were open, ready to be dropped on the necks of the horses and were fastened with snaps.*

The traces and holding back straps were attached to the fire wagon, leaving only the reins, the belly bands and the collars to be fastened.

The bridles were kept on the horses at all times except when they were being fed.

On each side of the building, beside the fire wagon, were stabled two beautiful gray horses, weighing about 1,500 pounds each. They were of the draft horse type, and the city paid $540 for the pair.

Though powerful animals, they had neither the speed nor endurance required to reach a distant fire quickly. So the "grays" were replaced with two "bays," which were bought at Fort Scott, Kansas.

These horses weighed about 1,300 pounds each but were much faster, and had greater endurance.

You see, they might be required to run as far as the Gibson Mill, a distance of two miles, pulling a heavy load, so speed was required as well as endurance.

Fire bell thrilled residents

"Never before nor since have the people of our community experienced a thrill equal to that of the fire alarm," wrote the author of the article.

The Courthouse bell would be rung rapidly and could be heard for miles; a large gong in the fire station would sound and the horses would prance as though they would tear out of their stable.

The "paid" fireman, Mr. Luther T. Byles, who was also the driver, quickly led the horses under the suspended harness which was deftly dropped on the animals and the collars, reins and belly bands were snapped and tightly fastened.

The doors were flung open on the sidewalk, and the team dashed out.

Volunteer firemen came running from all directions and swung onto the wagon, even though the horses were running at full speed.

Everyone had rushed out of the stores to see the thrilling sight.

If the fire occurred in the late afternoon, or at night, the thrill of sparks flying from the feet of the horses was added as their metal shoes struck the rocks on the unpaved street.

Our first fire wagon had plenty of real horsepower

In 1904, Concord was still a truly quiet, small but growing village. It could boast a number of cultural activities, electricity, some sidewalks, a few telephones, even a few water lines. But there was no fire department. The terror of fire—always a menace to be feared, even with today's sophisticated equipment and advanced skills—was ever present with our townsfolk then. In those days, most homes and businesses were heated by open fires, and a major cause of fire was sparks from a chimney landing on a shingle roof.

Before 1904, and at least as far back as 1898, our townsmen had been organized into firefighting teams who ran from home or business when someone screamed "fire" and the fire bell—the old courthouse bell, that is—started ringing.

Fire response so slow

These business and working people, before they could fight any fire, had to hitch up borrowed horses to borrowed wagons to haul firefighting equipment. After this slow start, they would race off at full speed to the scene of the blaze, an old newspaper clipping tells us. What their success rate was, no one knows. But in that time, those organized teams of amateur volunteers surely tried their best.

Well, in 1904, little Concord went modern, took a deep civic breath and went into the firefighting business. One can imagine the excitement the day two enormous, matched gray horses—John, named after Mayor John Caldwell, who spearheaded the fire department project, and Bill—trained to the utmost, arrived in town.

Trained fire horses marvel of the day

It isn't known where the horses came from, or who trained them, but these great animals were looked on as marvels of modern horse-training science of the day. They were quartered in special stalls in the town's new fire department—where the old city hall was located, directly across from the Historic Cabarrus Courthouse—and when the fire bell sounded, they pricked up their ears, snorted and danced around in their stalls.

The amazing part came when I.T. Biles, the town's first fire-wagon driver, opened their stall door. These two highly trained horses would race out of their stalls at full speed but come to a dead stop at a designated spot. Biles then would pull a rope, and the horses' harness would drop from the ceiling right over their backs. All Biles had to do was swiftly pull up the wagon and fasten the harness. The small but modern, streamlined fire wagon itself was loaded with hose, axes and other equipment, including chemicals carried in tanks underneath the wagon.

Firefighters soon found, however, that it sometimes took three men to keep the prancing horses from bolting to do their duty, until Biles could climb to the driver's seat. When they were finally released, their metal shoes sent sparks flying as they clattered across the sidewalk. The resulting sprint over the town's rough streets could be likened to the old chariot races of ancient Rome. They raced, bells clanging, dust or mud—depending on the weather—flying, chickens and children scattering, other horses hitched to other wagons shying away or trying to join the race. As the wagon careened along, the town's volunteer firemen jumped aboard and frantically held on. It all brought children and adults running to watch...for sure, in 1904, this was excitement along those quiet village roads.

But picture the same scene at night, as they made the dash along poorly lit village streets. Exciting, yes. And with fire, always frightening.

At the scene

For the firefighters, that was just the beginning. Arriving at the burning structure, some firemen grabbed the hose and ran to the fire while others took the other end of the hose and hooked it to the nearest hydrant—a blessing, as in areas that lacked water lines, the fire wagons had to carry their own water. In later years, the firemen turned their dousing efforts into fierce competitions. They organized fire teams from over the surrounding area and sponsored meets and competitions called fire conventions to determine which teams could get the greatest amount of water on a fire in the fastest time.

As can be imagined, those gray fire horses were a source of pride to all the town. They gave their all, the old clipping showed, but it was all too short a time, for after a few years, one of the horses simply dropped dead in his tracks. And by about 1916, not too long before the United States entered World War I, Concord's fire department took another giant stride, going motorized.

But in between, there were some significant fires, those dashing horses and some significant firefighters.

When the fire wagon raced to the Odell Mill inferno

Imagine the urgency, the pressure, that summer day in 1908 when Concord's small horse-drawn fire wagon heard the alarm bells clanging for J.M. Odell's mill. It was breaking into a fiery mass of flame!

Since the mid-1800s, Odell Mill had been the village's bread and butter. Its success had spun Concord into a dizzying cycle of growth and prosperity. The village's population swelled with new workers and myriad signs of progress—the establishment of new banks, the introduction of a horse-drawn trolley system, prospects of a city light and water department, and the birth of multiple areas of civic and cultural activities. And now the mill, the largest textile plant in the state, was burning! The whole town was fearful: with that fire could go all those jobs—some four hundred of them.

Now that model operation, which by the mid-1890s was drawing cotton people from everywhere to study its superlative operations, was about to burn to the ground. It had even brought the first electrical system to the town of Concord, dazzling citizens one night in 1888 when all its lights were first turned on.

When the courthouse bell rang the alarm on the night of the mill fire, you can be sure that old John and old Bill—the great gray horses that pulled the town fire wagon—followed their training process and made their customary mad dash to the scene. This time it was straight to the top of North Union Street, where towering flames could be seen. Firemen rode the wagon or ran on foot, with volunteers and townspeople joining them. This time, every bit of help was needed, for that one small horse-drawn fire wagon was the city's complete fire arsenal.

It is said that firefighters managed to save perhaps half of Odell Mill that fiery night.

Another setback: Concord suffered another nearly disastrous fire that summer of 1908, when Kerr Bleaching and Dyeing Company was struck by lightning during a torrential storm.

Kerr Bleachery had been of growing importance in the town's industrial network. Now consider what the fire-wagon driver (believed to have still been the first, I.T. Biles, that year) encountered as he steered the wildly racing horses down West Depot Street (now Cabarrus Avenue) that stormy night.

A close call

The driver, horses and firemen on the wagon were saved by a flash of lightning! Just in time, the flash illuminated a house sitting in the middle of the street; in the process of moving the house to another site, workmen had left it there when they couldn't finish the job that day. Biles was able to stop the charging horses and swiftly guide John and Bill around the house.

They sped on to the blaze, but to no avail. Rains had flooded the area around the textile processing plant, and firefighters couldn't get to the building. That structure burned to the ground. The Bleachery, however, was to recover and to continue its successful run in the town's industrial life for some sixty more years.

It is ironic that another fiery lightning bolt hit the bleachery in 1978.

Concord's first fire chief was J.L. Miller, who became one of the most durable men in this area's firefighting annals. He served the department for fifty-two years. City fire department records from that period are scanty, but they note that Cecil Foil succeeded Biles as fire-wagon driver.

Concord firemen competed well

Over the years, Concord firemen have performed often and well in big, competitive regional fire tests. In these "conventions," men and horses, formed into hose-and-reel companies, put their firefighting abilities to the test and vied for honors. As motorized equipment became more widespread, these competitions gradually disappeared. About eight years after the Odell Mill fire, around 1916, the city made a revolutionary and permanent change by purchasing its first motorized truck, first driven by R.M. Sappenfield and J.P. Peacock.

But some missed those magnificent horses. Years later, Fire Chief C.L. Miller—son of the first chief—was to sigh with regret. "When they took the horses out of firefighting," Miller said, "they took the fun out of it."

The August day when fire razed Odell Mill

August 15, 1908. Back then, it must have seemed a run-of-the-mill kind of day in the small village of Concord. The town had been enjoying a boom period. Odell Manufacturing Company, at the top of Union Street North, was running its big cotton mill industry. The newcomers, formerly poor farmers, not only earned a living but formed a mill village around Odell Mill. They even had their own church, Forest Hill Methodist, courtesy of Captain J.W. Odell—an outgrowth of his personal faith and his belief that religious people made good cotton mill workers.

Odell's mill was so meticulously planned and operated that textile people from all over the southeast came here to study his methods, reported historian Gary Freeze, who studied the Odells and the mill in depth.

Hotbox flames ignite mill

Anyway, that hot August day, about noon, flames from a hotbox flared near the elevator shaft and quickly brought a fire alarm signal. Employees fled. The town's volunteer firemen and the matched gray fire horses raced, bells clanging, to the scene, through the crowds of citizens running to watch. In less than an hour and a half, Concord's pride, the model mill, had burned to the ground. Here's how a local newspaper reported that catastrophe:

> *With great rapidity the flames spread, getting into the waste room where a large abundance of cotton added to the fuel, and in a very brief time, the entire building was full of fire.*
>
> *The fight to save the property was on. Water streams were turned on at every possible point* [in an] *effort to save what could be and to keep the flames from embracing the entire plant.*

Firefighters concentrated on the east end of the long building, which joined the other plants.

Firemen fought "gallantly"

According to the report, "Gallantly the firemen and others fought to keep the flames back and the exposed property from catching. All the water at hand was put to use, with all hoses turned on." It continued:

> *It was a matter of time and water. The contest was serious and intense. If the water held out, the chances were favorable* [for saving the building and preventing fire's spread].
>
> *In less than an hour the walls began to totter. Flames were bulging from every window and opening and the dense cloud of smoke went straight heavenward.*
>
> *Great throngs of spectators stood powerlessly by and with anxious hearts watched the fight raging* [between firemen and flames].
>
> *Pumps were running at full time, water was hurried from every available place. . . .*
>
> *The heat from a scorching noonday sun was terrific, and added to the discomfort from the heated building and many-tongued flames leaping from the doomed building.*
>
> *At one time it seemed as though the entire plant would go,* [but at 1:30 p.m., only one building had been lost].
>
> *Men, women and children stood about with sad faces watching the flames eating away into property worth more than half a million dollars.*

Bystanders wept

"Many wept. All along the streets stood crowds, settled down to accept the result," according to the report.

> *Loss estimates were not available, but Mill No. 4 "was a splendid structure, 125 feet long, by nearly 400 feet long, two stories high," with a basement where machinery was stored.*
>
> *On the first floor were looms, largely, while on the second floor were spindles and cards.*

> *The property destroyed must have been worth half a million dollars and was covered by insurance* [of around four hundred thousand dollars].

Machinery was also destroyed, but most manufactured goods were removed from the building, meaning only those being produced were lost to the fire.

Calm winds and firemen at every station—on the bridge connecting the buildings, on the roof and ground and everywhere else possible—helped save the remaining buildings. Apparently the sprinkler system either did not work or did not become operable quickly enough.

The article sized up the loss:

> *By this fire, something like a thousand people are thrown out of employment. This was the largest mill of the Odell plant and had been built for some 15 years. There were about 1,100 looms running in the building and from 30,000 to 40,000 spindles.*
>
> *There were about 200 looms in the basement....At present, estimates are that the loss will be about $450,000.*

For more than an hour business was practically suspended in the town, and the majority of the people, among them hundreds from the county, gathered around the burning building. "The great loss to the city is keenly felt on all sides and expressions of universal regret are to be heard everywhere," said the report.

Translate those losses into 1998 dollars, and it would be millions.

The fire seemed to be the beginning of the end for Odell Manufacturing Company. It never quite recovered, and eventually it went into bankruptcy. Indeed, it was a keen loss for little Concord for reasons never fully understood. But it did not end the town's rich textile heritage.

Fireworks store explodes in a blaze of glory

The day the fireworks store caught fire in 1908 in old downtown Concord was downright unforgettable. The scene: Union Street near the Historic Cabarrus Courthouse. One day in 1908, a big parade, the Fireman's Smoker, strode off at eight in the evening.

But first, a touch of history about the 1908 business district.

Old courthouse had columns

There were two round white columns on the Historic Cabarrus Courthouse's front entrance that long since have been torn away. In 1908, that proud courthouse was in its prime—just thirty-two years old. Around it were the old Allison, Litaker and Archey buildings.

The three-story Allison building still stood, on the corner of Union Street and Corban Avenue. On the first floor was Gus Hartsell's Wholesale Grocery, on the second floor, offices and on the third floor, the North Carolina National Guard Armory. It was demolished in the 1970s for the present county courthouse.

Across Union Street was the "new" city hall—an impressive 1903 building with a stone tower. (In the 1950s, it was demolished for a new, less dramatic city hall at Barbrick and Union Streets.) Adjoining the Allison building to the north was a smaller building that housed Cephus Litaker's printing business, Reed's Drug Store, Ritz's Fireworks Store and Ernest Shepherd's Shoe Hospital. Beside that, immediately beside the Historic Cabarrus Courthouse, was the Archey building, where Dr. J.A. Wallace (who married Dr. Archey's daughter, Helen) established and ran one of Concord's earliest hospitals. Today's courthouse occupies all the land those three buildings sat on while the restored Historic Cabarrus Courthouse still stands. Across the street, the Pythian building was just four years old.

In the parade were a horse and wagon, driven by Joe Y. Morrison, carrying a large American flag. Also in it were Concord policemen and firemen. The fire wagon was also in the procession. Driving the wagon was Cap Fisher, owner of a large livery stable at Church Street and St. Charles Avenue. Parade viewers also saw a fringed surrey, drawn by four mules, which carried the snappy Forest Hill Band.

Now we'll hear about the gigantic fireworks fire from an article in *Progress* magazine: "We believe that the date was Saturday, December 19, 1908, and the time about 7:30 p.m. that Ritz's Fireworks Store caught fire and became a blazing inferno in a very short time."

Roman candles, skyrockets, firecrackers

Here's how the article described the event:

> *The room was filled with a complete assortment of fireworks, intended for the Christmas trade. Included were caps, small firecrackers, giant firecrackers, sparklers, pin-wheels, sky rockets, Roman candles and on and on.*
>
> *The writer, then a boy of 15, was working at the Express Company during the Christmas holidays....*
>
> *The noise from the exploding firecrackers was deafening.*
>
> *Sparklers and pinwheels sputtered, sky rockets shot across Union Street, breaking windows upstairs in the building occupied by the Elk's Club, and Roman Candles, emitting varicolored balls of fire, illuminated this section of Concord as never before or since.*
>
> *Excitement reigned and the street and sidewalks were soon filled with men, women and children of all ages.*
>
> *Then the clanging of the fire bell as the fire wagons and the hose and reel carts arrived.*
>
> *The firemen, all volunteers, did a superb job and confined the fire to one-half of the Litaker building.*
>
> *By ten o'clock the fire was out and one could almost feel the quiet.*

What a gripping glimpse of a bit of excitement in quiet Concord many years ago.

Early Concord ball team smoked competition in summer 1911

Flushed with victories at Fort Mill [South Carolina], the Cinco team won another game Friday from Mount Pleasant, on the Graded School diamond, through the heavy slugging in the fifth which has characterized their recent games."

So we meet the Cincos of summer 1911, a team made up of nineteen young Concord men who are believed to have been the town of Concord's first baseball team. If you're a Concord or Kannapolis old-timer, you likely know many of their names. They played a nearly spectacular season in 1911—twenty games, with fourteen wins and six losses. Then some of the fellows went off to college.

This information comes to us thanks to Hank Utley, Concord's local baseball expert and author, who spent months tracking down information on the Cincos.

The Cincos got their strange name from a cigar, promoted and sold by A. Jones Yorke of Concord, a well-known merchant and distributor. Yorke, with a fifty-dollar donation from a Mr. Cannon, helped buy uniforms and equipment for the home team. There's a little tale about Jones Yorke's cigars: Seems he traveled much of the South, handing out sample cigars to men he encountered, sitting around chatting in stores. He'd also give them a nickel and tell them to buy another Cinco. That they'd do, and if the merchants didn't have Cincos, they'd soon order them.

But back to baseball!

A happy, winning summer

Newspaper accounts of the Cincos' heavy bats and other baseball exploits tell of a happy summer for the home team, in the characteristically colorful vernacular of those early sportswriters. In the Mount Pleasant game, according to one,

> *the Cincos started things off in the first when O. Sappenfield drove out a single, stole second while Grier puffed out. Patterson laced out a clean one, which went past the left and center fielders and "O" scored with Patterson on third, where he died....*
>
> [In] *the fifth, the Cincos lambasted the ball to all sides of the lot and proved too strong for Cauble's taste. Caldwell got a scratch, scoring Sappenfield. Dusenberry stole second and third and scored on a scratch hit by Norman, who also did the "Ty Cobb" act, stealing second and third.*
>
> *The Cincos added two more in the seventh, [which was] the last of the run-getting,* [as] *Lee Foil showed his prowess as a twirler....This ended the agony.*

Sluggers head for Kannapolis

Then in August 1911, the team headed seven miles north. "The Cinco baseball team journeyed to Kannapolis and returned with another scalp of the YMCA ball tossers dangling from their belts." This news account, incidentally, was accompanied by a cartoon of a baseball player being hit in the stomach with a baseball, with a caption underneath: "Dusenberry took a siesta in left field and while [he was] peacefully communing with the fairies of slumberland, a Kannapolis slugger swatted the sphere straight to his tummy."

As to those Fort Mill games, well, the Cincos took two of a three-game series with the South Carolina nine. "The first game was a wretched farce on the part of the home boys, with seventeen errors of every kind and description chalked up against them, due partly to the fast diamond, partly to lack of sleep and partly to the thermometer taken along as a mascot."

In the second Fort Mill game, the batting and base running were "magnificent," the sportswriter said—eight runs, six hits and a walk in the fifth added up to a final score of 9 to 7 for the Cincos.

Thermometer a mascot?

The Cincos won the third game 6 to 3. "Everybody decided that the hoodoo of the first game was the thermometer which was hurled unmercifully to the ground just after the [initial] defeat." Well, I never figured out how a thermometer became a mascot—if that's what it was.

Now, just who were those nineteen young Concordians on that 1911 team? They were Charley Barrier, infield; Leslie Bell, pitcher; Ray Bell, manager; Bill Bingham, outfield; Ross Cannon, pitcher; Clark [first name unknown], outfield; Campbell Cline, pitcher; Pearlie Cook, outfield; Gowan Dusenberry, outfield; Grier [first name unknown], first base; Paul Means, pitcher; Clarence Norman, right field; Fred Patterson, catcher; Rogers [first name unknown], catcher; Luke Sappenfield, shortstop; Oscar Sappenfield, second base; Smith [first name unknown], catcher; Bill Wadsworth, centerfield and Wood [first name unknown], shortstop.

Ross Cannon, incidentally, was a brother of textile genius Charles A. Cannon, and Leslie Bell's brother-in-law was the late great U.S. senator Sam Ervin of Morganton. And the Grier fellow? He's believed to be the son of Dr. John Grier, once a pastor at Concord's First Presbyterian Church.

1911 Cincos at home on diamond and in Concord

Those young Cincos were a fascinating group of young men in a time when baseball was truly the national pastime, who came from all walks of life and were bonded by a shared love of baseball. Campbell Cline was a tall, rangy young pitcher who lived at 44 Corban Street East. Cline later became an agent with Creditors Protective Agency. I remember interviewing him years ago.

The Cincos shortstop, Wood, lived at 145 Vance Street. He was, Utley decided, either John Wood, a guard for the county chain gang, or Turvie Wood, a local clerk. Oscar Sappenfield, who played second and third base, either owned or worked in a local drugstore, Utley said. Oscar's brother Luke Sappenfield was also a shortstop. He was a clerk and lived at 16 Spring Street North.

Bill Wadsworth, the centerfielder, lived at 100 Union Street North. He later became a physician and surgeon. He was gassed during World War I and died young, Utley said. Charley Barrier played in the infield. He lived at 31 Corban Street West and went to Catawba College. He then had a short professional baseball career, but after his father died, he had to leave baseball to go to work. He was employed at the old Lippard and Barrier Grocery.

Gowan Dusenberry, who played in the outfield and also pitched, may have been among the more successful of the players. Dusenberry went to Suwanee College and later became president and manager of Gowan Medical Company. The company produced Gowan's Rub-It-On. Probably, Utley said, it was a patent medicine product. Outfielder Clark—whose first name eluded Utley—was among seven Clarks listed in the 1916–17 town telephone directory. All, Utley said, worked in local mills.

Bill Bingham was an outfielder. He lived at 80 North Georgia Avenue. Bingham later became a pharmacist for the old Gibson Drug Store on the square in downtown Concord. And Grier, first baseman, is believed to have been the son of Dr. John Grier, who in 1911 was pastor of Concord's First Presbyterian Church.

Leslie Bell was another Cincos pitcher. He and his brother Ray, who was manager of the team, lived at 100 West Depot Street. Leslie Bell later operated Bell Music Store for a number of years. Their sister married North Carolina's esteemed U.S. senator Sam Ervin of Morganton. Paul Means, who later became a lawyer, was a pitcher.

Clarence Norman played right field. He went to the University of North Carolina and later earned his living as a bookkeeper. There was a catcher named Rogers, and another catcher named Smith, but Utley was unable to determine the first name of either. Ross Cannon was a sensational pitcher. More about him in a bit.

There was, in one of the sports stories of 1911, a Cinco player whose last name was Caldwell. I am interested, because the player could be my father, Eugene, or his brother, Brice, or one of my cousins, Kenneth or Harry Caldwell. I hope someday to solve that puzzle.

Ross Cannon: "Sensational" pitcher

Now as to Ross Cannon, who pitched for the Locke Mill team, a 1911 sportswriter wrote glowingly of him:

> *Ross Cannon took a baseball and eight teammates, only one of whom was needed, and by flinging that ball with such force that it sped with such rapidity that only an occasional fleeting glimpse could be caught of it, and a wee small glimpse it was, and defeated North Charlotte 5 to 0.....*
>
> *Cannon's sensational pitching was about all there was to the defensive side of the game, although he received good support from his teammates on the few occasions they offered to assist him....The whole team played a fast and snappy game.*

Ross Cannon struck out eighteen batters.

Cincos baseball kept Concord cheering

What happened after that smoking winning record in the hot, dry summer of 1911? No one has researched that yet, according to Hank Utley, who's known for having a ball researching early baseball. "But [Concordian] Ed Morrison believes the team played at least two or three seasons," he said. "And Pat Ritchie told me he remembers, as a child, hearing his dad talk about the Cincos."

In 1911, baseball was the national pastime. Local folks attended games in throngs.

Citizens rebel against Cincos supporters

On game days, so many horse-drawn buggies trotted down the dirt road to the Cincos diamond, on Oakland Avenue off South Union Street, that neighbors began to bristle.

Together, they appeared before town aldermen. "Either run a trolley line down that road or oil it," they demanded, for the area was choking in buggy dust. I'd bet today that the city fathers oiled the road.

Another humorous, if fractious, episode stemmed from a local newspaper's sports write-up of one game between the Cincos and the Kannapolis YMCA. The newspaper described the game as "slow and uninteresting." The Concord nine, it seems, defeated Kannapolis, but in turn, Saturday, the next day, Concord was defeated by the Towel City team.

Irate Umpire

Now, even the umpire managed to get into things. Umpire Boger (first name unknown) took umbrage at the previous description of a game and fired off a snappish letter to the editor. It read:

> *Mr. Editor: Someone writing in Saturday's* [*Concord Daily*] *Tribune gives a very unfeeling account of the game.*
>
> *The writer must be a rooter for a metropolitan league team, possibly of New York, or Chicago or Philadelphia, where the players are professionals of the highest type, drawing princely salaries.*
>
> *Therefore he is too much of a critic to enjoy amateur playing when possibly some of the players are not yet in practice.*
>
> *It seems to your scribe that the criticism was unjust, but as for the game being "uninteresting" we would not expect it to interest anyone used to high professionals, and as to its being a "slow" game we do not know what he would call a fast game, but feel sure that the Cincos did not find the game Saturday evening so "uninteresting" when the YMCA boys made three doubles and so easily reversed the score of the day before, making it 9 to 4.*
>
> *Perhaps the game was so "slow" Friday that the Cincos were smoked rather short, causing their fire to die out rather early in Saturday's game.*
>
> *Our boys are smoking ten-cent cigars now, for they say Cincos are too cheap. This game was played on the Y.M.C.A. diamond. Game called at 3:10. Time: 1 hour 55 minutes.*

It was signed, "Umpire Boger." So the umpire had the final public word—as usual!

Bridge sometimes left travelers high, but not dry

For early Concord residents traveling to Midland, in buggies or old-time cars, curvy old Thunderstruck Bridge over Rocky River always looked safe as they approached it, despite torrential downpours and flooding. The old wooden bridge, believed to have been built before 1850, curved steeply upward and over that sometimes deep and swift Cabarrus river, and unwary travelers couldn't see to the other side.

For some reason, Rocky River's floodwaters never rose over the Concord side at Thunderstruck Bridge, said John Sharpe Hartsell of Hartsell, Hartsell and Mills law firm and Cabarrus native. So these folks would sometimes start across, reach the crest of the bridge, and then see high floodwaters swamping the other bank.

Double trouble on the bridge

"That's where they'd get in trouble," said Hartsell, during the first of several interviews aimed at compiling a store of little-known but intriguing bits of Cabarrus history. For in the middle of that arched bridge, they had to stop, and they couldn't turn around, Hartsell said. Imagine trying to turn or back a horse and buggy or an old Model T down that steep bridge with floodwaters raging below, he mused.

Naturally, some of those early folks ended up floating down the Rocky River. But living nearby, "back in the teens or early twenties," Hartsell recalled, was a gentleman named D.B. McCurdy—undoubtedly some relation to Cabarrus County's intrepid Revolutionary War hero Captain Archibald McCurdy. Sometimes during flood times,

McCurdy would hear frantic screams for help from the river and he'd dash over to attempt a rescue.

"I remember my mother describing one time when he went to help, and saw the people already in the water," Hartsell said.

McCurdy's help rescue

"Mother said Mr. McCurdy called out, 'I'll swim in and help you get out, if you won't all pile on me at once,'" Hartsell recalled, chuckling. But in all the years the curvy wooden Thunderstruck Bridge spanned Rocky River, Hartsell said, he never heard of anyone drowning there.

The name Thunderstruck Bridge stemmed from the fact that the bridge was once struck by lightning. It spanned Rocky River at a point several miles almost due south of Concord, on old Thunderstruck Bridge Road, which today we know as Flowe's Store Road, Hartsell said. Thunderstruck differed from other early crude bridges across Rocky River and other major creeks and streams that crisscross Cabarrus, as it rose higher than the river. Other bridges were built from one bank to the opposite bank, just above the water. As a result, the bridges were regularly swept away during heavy rains and floods. Thunderstruck Bridge, however, did not disappear until 1938, Hartsell said, and for many years it was one of the major river-crossing points for county farmers and travelers.

Modern drivers zip across Rocky River on a high and substantial bridge, with nary a thought of those ancient waters beneath. All along Rocky River's meandering route through the county, though, there's legend and lore.

Sometimes navigable, sometimes not

Rocky River is a familiar, historic watercourse, sometimes navigable by canoe for much of its length. It enters northwest Cabarrus County, ambles southward toward Harrisburg and then makes a sharp turn east toward Mount Pleasant. From there it runs southeastward, further on forming the boundary between Stanly and Anson Counties. Along the way, the river widens, gathers steam and then empties into the Pee Dee River.

Early pioneers, however, waded or swam across the river, before the advent of those first simple spans across it. The earliest bridges were at Black's Mill and at Pharr's Mill, both near Rocky River Presbyterian Church.

There's another important factor centering on Rocky River as well as other county waterways. In early days here, when heavy rains sent Rocky River waters out of its banks, our pioneers often faced trying situations. Old Rocky wasn't a river you could trifle with when it got to rolling in flood times. It meant farmers and travelers waded or swam across it at considerable peril.

"In harvest times, when the farmers were trying to get their vegetable wagons to market—down to Fayetteville or Camden—they just had to turn around, go home and can them instead," said Hartsell, longtime a student of area history.

Three early fords helped

Travelers could choose from at least two shallow fords—Bost Ford, near old Bost Mill, southwest of Concord, and Hagler Ford, named for the Hagler home place nearby—through which to cross the river, Hartsell said. The Hagler river crossing was also near the T.J. Shinn home.

Today it may be hard to realize how much of early Cabarrus life—for both the work and the pleasure of our pioneers—centered, even depended, on the Rocky River. Citizens fished there, drew water, swam, waded and gathered for picnics along its banks. Homes were built beside or near it. Also along the river's winding route were many little mills for grinding grains, many of which later became attractive gathering places for early Cabarrus folk.

"It is really amazing how many mills Cabarrus County had," Hartsell said. He mused a spell and added: "It is also interesting to note how fascinated people have always been with rivers and streams."

Those gristmills

Among the most popular mills was Bost Mill, which today still stands after more than two hundred years. In early years the Bost Mill had a dam, which backed the waters into a good-sized pond, Hartsell said.

"People from Concord, back in the teens and twenties, would drive down there in their horse and buggies and swim and picnic.

"Mr. E.T. Bost Sr., who owned Bost Mill, provided some rowboats for the lake, and he'd let the community boys row young couples on boat rides—for a small charge—during their picnics."

Chuckling, Hartsell recalled an elderly man who once paid his fare, plopped himself into one of the boats—and firmly sat there the entire afternoon, trip after trip after trip, without paying additional fare. "He wouldn't get out. He just kept on riding," Hartsell said. Finally the young oarsman paddled the boat quite close to the eight-foot-high dam, turned it around and positioned it so the old fellow was sitting square over the rushing waterfall. "That old gentleman was ready to get out when they got back to shore," Hartsell said.

So popular was Bost Mill that even when people had cars, they'd still drive to Bost Mill, "especially on Wednesday afternoon, when all the stores in Concord closed," Hartsell said. (I remember parents of some of my friends, here in Concord, recalling those days and the time when they were picnicking there and one of their young friends drowned while swimming.)

Fourth of July shindig

Rocky River boasted other popular mill sites, Hartsell said, especially Garmon's Mill at Midland in southern Cabarrus County, where a rousing Fourth of July shindig was a tradition. "The young blades would rent a livery stable horse and buggy to take their girlfriends down to Garmon's, which also had a lake," he recalled. "There weren't any electric refrigerators, but you could always bank on Henry G. Ritz being there with his lemonade stand."

"He was a merchant in Concord, and he always took three stands [barrels] of homemade ice cream on his wagon. They were like big five-gallon ice cream freezers, packed in ice.

"And he always had candy and gum and cigars, and varieties of all kinds—and balloons."

Pharr's Mill still standing

Still another popular Rocky River site was Pharr's Mill, according to Hartsell, which still is remembered for a double tragedy: long ago, young twin brothers drowned there, simultaneously. Though much weathered today, the mill still stands on its original site. So it is that early Rocky River was both a blessing and sometimes a bane.

Early colonists, in days when wells were hard to come by, depended on Rocky River for their water, as well as Coddle Creek and Irish-Dutch Buffalo Creek and the countless little streams, creeks and rivulets that run their courses over Cabarrus County. They drew the streams' water, fished them for food and during the hot summers cooled themselves in their currents.

Mule Floats Down River

Those early folk also savored the humorous incidents—long told, long remembered. "I recall my father telling about the time he was coming home from Albemarle and had to cross Big Bear Creek, which was flooding," Hartsell said. "There was this fellow there with a small mule and a wagon, debating whether to cross the creek or not, and my father stopped and asked the fellow if he thought it was all right to cross. The fellow told him, 'I suppose so,' but added, 'You have a bigger horse, you go first.' Well, my father got across it all right, but when the fellow tried it, that little mule went floating down the creek like an empty barrel."

What great stories the Rocky River has given us!

Sam Goodman's opera nights were special once

This essay emerges from 1920s or 1930s Concord, and it centers on the inimitable Sam Goodman, a local tenor, teacher, promoter, and eccentric singer and lover of opera and other classical music. Sam and his sister Miss Addie Goodman lived in an extravagant Spanish-style hacienda on Gold Hill Road, complete with arched windows, ironwork doors, statues, a great organ, fountains and hound dogs. The property was adorned with lilacs, lily ponds and plum trees. Also there was Sam's heifer, Madame Butterfly....

My good fortune is that my sister-in-law and late brother-in-law Edith and Don Arthur owned that house after Mr. Sam and Miss Addie passed on to their great reward, and they saved a wonderful old column about Sam from an early Concord daily newspaper. Unfortunately, there's no date on it, but the clipping is yellowed.

I remember going with my music-teacher mother, Lena Caldwell, to one of Mr. Sam's musical evenings. I recall he played the organ and played some opera on an ancient phonograph and explained each segment as the hound dogs roamed all around him. I, of course, was more interested in the hound dogs at that time.

Area music lovers adored Sam and Addie, and his operatic evenings brought out most of them. Those evenings provoked a lot of, um, well, memories, surprises and excitement. The yellowed clipping is titled "Cheery Chatter," and the signature at the end was simply "Meda." I never heard of Meda, but he or she was one heck of a writer. "We drove up a winding road, up a steep hill to a Spanish house where we were to listen to an evening of *Carmen*," Meda began.

"It sounds like a story book, doesn't it? But it's as real as air and water."

The ultimate romantic Spanish villa?

"The Spanish house was there in all its original entirety, complete with its niches where madonnas in flowing robes stood, with its arched windows, its doors of iron railing, its step-ups and step-downs between rooms," the article continued.

"Its Spanish fireplace, its open courtyard, its stepping stones and lily pond."

And, of course—what country home is complete without them?—its flop-eared dogs.

> *When you go to Miss Addie's and Sam Goodman's home, you are transformed into another world.*
>
> *Thursday, listening to* Carmen *being played, I confess I did not try to depict the opera.*
>
> *Sam explained each scene and each piece of music to his guests, but I was watching the adorable doors and little gates and visioning things other than opera; things such as women in white lace skirts flirting with Spanish caballeros.*
>
> *I envisioned romance and under the moon in the open patio where the lily pond lay, as Carl Sandburg would say, "Like a wide dreaming pansy."*

Perfect wedding venue

"With my eyes fixed on a candelabra in corner of the living room, I thought of a wedding. What a beautiful setting for a wedding!" wrote Meda.

> *I could picture someone in eggshell lace with her hair covered by a lace mantilla that fell to the floor and spread like a fan when she walked.*
>
> *I could smell the perfume of orange blossoms and gardenias, and exquisite green orchids.*
>
> *Even as the famous "Toreadora Song" was being played, I pictured tiny golden wedding rings on white satin pillows, tiny golden wedding rings in the hearts of roses.*
>
> *During the play of "Habanera," my mind dwelled upon the thing I've always remembered when I hear that particular song.*
>
> *In the days of the silent pictures, when movies furnished their own music by using self-players, I saw a movie made from Gene Stratten Porter's last movie,* The Magic Garden.
>
> *I remember a little golden-haired girl, sitting on the bank of a stream, getting ready to wade in the water.*

It gets better and better.-Frankly, I think the writer had to be a woman. Don't know many men who would think along those lines—but there probably are some, somewhere.

Anyway, the early *Tribune* columnist continued to compare the scene to a silent movie she had seen. She wrote, "I remember a little golden-haired girl, sitting on the bank of a stream," in a woodsy yet pastoral setting, "with big Amaryllis lilies, striped tiger lilies and tall blades of grass."

"The movie, blindly furnishing its own music for the scene, played 'Habanera.' I can't get away from it," she continued.

As Sam played operatic numbers on his very own pipe organ, "The notes of music seemed to drift lightly among the plum blossoms and lilacs."

"I thought of hedges in the rain, of wet roses, of newly-cut grass," Meda wrote.

Hounds mingle with guests

Meanwhile, there went Sam's hounds, mingling with the guests. "Circling in and out slowly and almost with rhythmic tread among the guests was red Irish setter Patsy, the long hair on her ears almost curly, her eyes shining and brown and almost human in their appeal," the columnist wrote.

> *Jack, the larger of the setters, did not put in an appearance until later in the evening.*
>
> *Then with an air of mastery and self pride, he strutted among the guests, sniffing the toes of their shoes inquiringly and then ready to amble on after a brief pat on the head.*
>
> *Came refreshment time, and Sam picked up Patsy, her red floppy ears lolling against Sam's shoulder, and carried her bodily out.*
>
> *While we were roasting wieners on the porch and spreading them thick with mustard, both the flop-eared dogs put in an appearance.*
>
> *They were mannerly and did not try to sniff at the table or put their paws up on it.*

Dogs add their own music

Our writer then digressed.

> *Miss Addie and Sam took Jack and Patsy to Myrtle Beach with them last week-end.*
>
> *Arriving, they found their cottage rented by their agent to a group of people from the North. So Miss Addie and Sam and Jack and Patsy went to a hotel.*
>
> *Jack and Patsy were put in a room in the basement, but after an hour's time, they decided that the basement room was too confining.*
>
> *They both proceeded to scratch heavily on the door, accompanying it with melodious whines.*

Jack and Patsy were taken to the automobile and put inside. For about an hour they were content enough, thinking every moment that someone would come along and take them for a ride.

Upon discovering that no such ride was forthcoming, they used their nails and vocal cords again to advantage.

This time they were taken into a bedroom of the hotel where they seemed content enough.

Next day, some people at the hotel said, "Didn't a couple of people have some dogs with them?"

Sam said, "No, a couple of dogs had some people with them."

This colorful column was signed simply "Meda." (It seems to me I got a note from someone saying Meda was a local woman, named Armstrong, but I haven't confirmed this.)

More on Sam

I have more to tell you about Sam and his music, thanks to Guy Beaver Jr., who loaned me his scrapbook on Goodman. Believe me, it is loaded with good stuff. Did you know, for instance, that Goodman served in the army during World War I? But first, he pursued a singing career.

Our Sam Goodman sang opera in New York City

"A hometown boy goes to New York to study voice, which was almost unheard of in Concord. All of Sam's friends were excited, as well as his family." That Sam, you surely know, was our Sam Goodman, a genuine character who wore many hats during his colorful, philanthropic and humor-filled lifetime. "As the story goes," wrote "Miss Elma" Beaver—Guy's mother, who gave a talk on Sam for the Sidney Lanier Book Club years ago—"Sam Goodman had a friend, Mr. Robert Phifer."

Robert Phifer grew up in a brick colonial home in Concord, where First Presbyterian Church now stands. He went to New York, added to the Phifer fortune through stocks and real estate and came to appreciate grand opera. Phifer also accumulated a collection of fine art and ultimately gave $1.5 million worth of his paintings to the North Carolina Museum of Art in Raleigh.

Somewhere, Phifer had heard Sam Goodman, who had a superb tenor voice, sing, Elma Beaver wrote. So, on one of his usual fall trips to Concord to enjoy golfing and hunting, Phifer invited Goodman to study voice under a noted teacher, Oscar Sanger, in New York at Phifer's expense.

1918: He enlists in the army

Young Goodman accepted Phifer's offer, but while he was in New York, the United States entered World War I. He quickly enlisted in the army and soon after sailed for France with the Sixth Division. He sent his mother, Margaret Biles Goodman, a cryptic card: "Arrived safely overseas, Sam." That's all it said.

Not too much is known about Goodman's military service, but a down-to-earth sense of humor emerged when he wrote a friend that he was a member of the "Sightseeing Sixth in France" that traveled all over that country.

After the war, Sam's singing career took off, and he performed roles in grand opera. On April 11, 1922, he wrote a local friend, Mrs. Howard Caldwell:

> *I am getting ready to make my debut next month in "Pagliacci," with an opera company here in New York that plans to give six weeks of Italian opera.*
>
> *The chorus from the Metropoliton* [sic] *will be used, and all the principals will be Italian or French except poor me and the donkey.*
>
> *I hope the donkey doesn't balk when I make my entrance.*
>
> *I am planning to sing on the radio phone next month at Newark Broadcasting station. Do the radio phones there pick up Newark? If they do, I will let you know the exact date. Yours Very Truly.*

A local legend

Sam Goodman explored New York with enthusiastic thoroughness while he was performing with the Metropolitan Opera, more than eighty years ago. Once, "Going to the Catholic cathedral," Elma Beaver told the Sidney Lanier Book Club, "he encountered a wedding party with all their evening finery and showers of orchids."

"He asked a [church] employee if it were an important wedding. He said 'no,' it couldn't be very important, or they wouldn't have it at that hour of the day. Sam," Elma Beaver continued, "thought he would write Emily Post about that."

"Sam planned on going to the *Hour of Organ Music* at St. Thomas' Church, where a world-famous organist and composer [Tertious Noble] gave a recital every Sunday evening, but his shoes were full of snow, and some of it was melting, so he had to go back to his hotel and dry out before catching the train for home."

Guy Beaver Jr.'s colorful scrapbook on Goodman has many pictures of him in his World War I uniform.

Mother ill; Sam leaves opera

After Sam's mother became ill, he gave up opera and returned home, but "he visited New York often during the opera season," Elma Beaver wrote.

"While there he always visited the magnificent churches to hear the great organs and the wonderful choirs," and there he also often went with friends to Lindy's for supper after the operas. "He saw women in their new flowered spring hats, [and] as it was snowy outside he said the snow on the flowers looked funnier than the spring hats this time of year."

Sam Goodman visited most of those grand churches in New York, including the Russian Orthodox cathedral, which had no pews and where worshipers stood or knelt during the long services. Well, Sam Goodman leaned against the wall during that service. A church official invited him to the Christmas service, which began at seven in the evening and continued until midnight.

He also visited St. Bartholomew, which then was described as "the richest congregation in the world." Sam thought it had the finest choir. His humor again: Sam said if they had charged ten dollars to hear that choir, instead of allowing visitors in for free, the church would overflow, "as it was much better than some of the operas produced in New York."

Builds Myrtle Beach cottage

"After his mother's death," Miss Elma's program continued, "Sam purchased a lot in Myrtle Beach and built a summer home there, where he and sister Addie spent much time.

"They had many Concord friends down for summer visits. He later sold this home."

Miss Elma continued:

> *I remember well his two Irish setter dogs riding in the back seat of his Cadillac. Sam's pride and joy was his heifer named Madame Butterfly.*
>
> *Back in the silent movie days, Sam liked to attend theaters to hear the organ and self-player pianos. After the coming of "talking pictures," theaters no longer needed organs.*
>
> [So] *Sam bought one of the movie theater organs and placed it in the new Spanish-type home he had built on Gold Hill Road.*
>
> *He often gave "musicals" for visitors, and friends would bring their own drums and horns, and together they would entertain the neighbors.*

Sam continued to foster local music programs

But there was much more to Sam Goodman's love of music. "In 1944, Sam began giving vocal scholarships through the N.C. Federation of Music Clubs. Each winner gave a recital following his/her summer at *Juilliard* [Conservatory of Music] at Sam's home [named Buenhombre]. Some 30 youths were scholarship recipients. Often they were star performers." On coming home, Sam was tenor soloist for years at First Presbyterian Church in Concord and also served as organist there.

Born December 27, 1885, he died sixty-nine years later, on October 15, 1954. Miss Addie continued his scholarship program, "as a memorial to him," until she died in 1967. Neither Sam nor Miss Addie ever married, and on Miss Addie's death, the remainder of his estate went to charitable institutions, including Cabarrus Memorial Hospital (now NorthEast Medical Center), which was given a grant of sixty-five thousand dollars—a goodly sum in the 1960s—and half-interest in a house he owned on Georgia Avenue in Concord.

North Carolina music federation pays tribute

Upon Goodman's death, the North Carolina Federation of Music Clubs, at a meeting in Lincolnton, paid silent tribute to this man of the arts, who contributed so much of his time and money to promoting music, opera and young musicians.

"At one time," declared an article in an old *Concord Daily Tribune*, "Mr. Goodman gave a musical vespers at 6 p.m. daily at his home, [and] a loudspeaker built on the outside of the house carried the music for miles." What a lovely way to share a lifetime of musical love!

A state federation spokesman's comment could apply to a wide area in these parts, on Goodman's death: "Certainly the federation has lost a true friend and a fine musician."

Patt Covington wrote saucy ads to sound like chatty letters

"COme to COvington's, COncord, N.C."

"Here ye are! Here ye are! / Same old store; same old stand; / Same old price; same old plan / —that's Patt." We're in for some fun reading, courtesy of the late Patt Covington, who in the 1920s and 1930s ran a candy, variety and secondhand store in downtown Concord.

Ran it, that is, until the cyclone of 1937 came along and blew the First Presbyterian Church steeple across the elegant backyard of "Miss Emma" Cannon, laid trees low all over town and reduced Patt's little variety store to a heap of rubble. After that, I've heard, he moved to Albemarle.

But until that ripsnorter hit the town (I recall stepping over fallen trees and power lines while walking to Coltrane School that day), C. Patt Covington had a ball writing his wry, witty, down-home ads for the local newspapers. These homespun gems of long-ago advertising—some as early as 1925—were clipped and put into a scrapbook by the late June Hoover, wife of the late Gene Hoover of Concord.

Native Concordian Hank Utley recalled that Covington's candy store first was located on Church Street South but later moved to Barbrick Street near a livery stable. (I thought I was an expert on early Concord candy stores but just don't recall that one.)

A sampling of advertising gems

Now I will give you a sampling of Patt Covington's little advertising gems. Unfortunately, there are no dates on any of them, nor is there any indication in which paper they were printed. Here goes:

*"*Patt, like the cat, comes back to Barbrick Street. Thirty years older, twice as deaf and lame, but otherwise the same.*

He wants to sell you two book cases, books, pictures and second stuff, shoe laces, shoe polish and 3-8 tacks, large cook pots, small wash pans, men's coats, little girl coats and cane bottom chairs.

Like Mayor Barrier, I am the Same Old Man at the Same Old Stand. C. Patt Covington."

*"*We have just gotten in 15 odd coats, 10 overcoats, $3.00, $3.50, $4.00, sizes up to 48; all dark colors and worn..."*

*"*I had an understanding with the Almighty that I'd treat people right if I ever got well, but being naturally a little inclined to be shady, you are invited to watch me. So get at it at once. Yours for business, C. Patt Covington."*

*"*Close out shoes 50 pair; hammer and hatchet handles, 3 for 25; buttons 10 cards for 10; stove polish, stove pans and elbows, 20 each; oil lamps, solid brass burner, 65."*

*"*The graces are four / The muses are nine, / There's only one Cleo / and that one is mine." Wow!*

*"*How silly for a man of my age! Uncle Pete...says he loaned his pastor $50 to buy food and clothing for his family but the preacher took the money and made a down payment on a secondhand car and forgot the loan. Hoping you'll not forget me. C. Patt Covington."*

*"*I'm a poor old lonely Bozo / No better half is mine / No wife to tell me so and so / Or raise the devil with me / When I misbehave / I'm a poor old lonely Bozo."*

*"*Just received 10-quart white slop jars $1.00 each; mixed screws 10 [cents?] a pound...and remember the dollar coats for girls and little women, warm and good enough for Sunday school and cheap enough for everyday wear."*

Let's hear 'em sing!

*"*I'd like to hear Sam Goodman, Mrs. J.B. Womble [my aunt!], Kay Patterson, Mrs. C.B. Wagoner and Ed Sherrill sing the Fanny Crosby hymns over the radio. It would put the old town on the map.*

The best singing I ever heard in Concord was by these five. Let's have some singing that's called music.

Yours with a bum leg, C. Patt Covington."

*"*Four secondhand liquor jugs; three secondhand book cases; twenty secondhand chairs and also beds, cots, books, tables, pictures and etc. Going, going, gone."*

*"*Miss Cot,* The Tribune's *lady philosopher, says milk isn't good for folks, but I'm selling lots of four-gallon milk buckets for 50 each and strainers for 25 each; women's old style shoes, 50; two-strap gaiters, $2 pair; men's hats, coats, overcoats and suits, $1 to $10 each. Come gettum."*

*"Jim Ray says for me to lay off all mother-in-law jokes; says he kisses his mother-in-law regular as the clock works and likes it, too.

Well, I'll be durned, who'd-a thunk it? Clocks, $1; Gillette blades 5 a box; paper, tablets, pencils.

Come and look. Yours, till death us do part. C. Patt Covington."

*"Faith and bejabbers, my heart is plain broke! 'Twas just since Christmas I fell in love with the sweetest little lady you ever saw and last Sunday she ran off to South Carolina and married another man.

Begosh, I'm plum through with the heartbreaking adorable things forever. I'm gonna tend my store and see if I can't get well.

And never mind about that mule; I've had enough kicking already.

N. B. I just got in a lot of buckets, dippers, bakers, clothes pins, rolling pins, chair seats in all sizes, small stew pots, dairy pails and rotary flour sifters, sailors' white caps 30 each; little girls' dollar hats 10 each; men's top coats $3.00 each, sack coats $2.50. I plum forgot the price on ladies' shoes and overshoes. Kumgettum.

You gotta stop kicking my dog around. C. Patt Covington.

Can you believe all that? The imagination of that man. Read on.

Genuine American original

Patt Covington surely would qualify as a genuine American original. Here's more of his folksy writing during those pre-World War II Depression years: "I'm like old Dr. Rowe, former pastor of Central Methodist Church," Covington wrote in a Concord newspaper ad sixty or so years ago. "He used to say that he had no desire to go to heaven as long as he could serve God and preach the gospel in Concord.

"That's me; if I can serve the people in Concord, I don't want to go to heaven.

"If you have anything your family has outgrown, come in, trot it out; I'll buy, swap or sell."

Continuing this ad, Covington advertised a cookstove, heater, bed, cot, four tables, twenty chairs, two rockers, one bookcase, oil lamps, burners, chimneys, buckets, dippers, wash pans and slop jars—and then added: "And if I don't get to selling something pretty soon, I think I'll start a country school and teach young ladies how to make bashful lovers hug, kiss and propose and not even think about it. Yours, till I get married."

Then there was this one:

"For sale: Minor and Moore's business arithmetics and Gregg shorthand books... [both for $1.50]*, and a cast iron pot and kettle, slightly used dutch oven and lid, quilting frames, shoe tacks [$.05 each], and 10¢ and 15¢ novelties."*

"I've moved into my store, bag and baggage, and eat and sleep here. I'm going to stay here as long as I live and be buried under the floor when I die. C. Patt Covington."

*"I'm plumb discouraged with the women. I hired one, she gets engaged to a young man and went to work for him.

I hired another she got married and yet I hired another, she got drunk and got in jail, that finished me. I'm through with the disagreeable things."

> **"Coats, coats, for girls and women $1 each, good as they ever were. Coffee cups and cream pitchers 10c each."*

> **"Hoover democrats you know a Hoovercrat wants the whole world with a fence around it for a nickel. Well, I hope you don't do like uncle Peter Foster, forget. Yours truly, C. Patt Covington."*

That same week Covington also wrote he had frying pans for fifteen cents, wall lamps and tin reflectors for fifty cents and "good spectacles strong enough for anybody to see a job with, 25c a pair."

> **"I dreamed that I died and went to hell last night and saw the devil with a derby hat on like I sell for $1. I asked the devil why he had no fire and he told me he had all kinds of hell for all sorts of people.*
>
> *I then noticed a great crowd of people that I owed money in this world and when I tried to dodge them I ran into an even greater throng and I felt so mean I asked the devil about a plan to dodge my creditors and he said it can't be done; you are in hell now because you failed to pay your honest debts up above.*
>
> *Then I socked the devil in the jaw but hit my bedpost and waked up and the devil still had my hat like I sell for $1.00. Also dishes and bowls, paper and envelopes at 25c—bargain! City hall block...C. Patt Covington."*

That same day Covington wrote he also had "a big lot of ladies' overcoats, mostly with fur collars, price $3.00 and $4.00. Ladies' hats, 49c...and shoe polish, black, brown and tan, 10c."

Customer remembers shopping at Covington's

B.H. Dry of Kannapolis called to tell me of an encounter he had with that wag C. Patt Covington.

"Patt Covington was a real comic," Dry said. "I remember going in his store one time, when I was maybe twelve or thirteen years old. He told me he'd waited on a hundred customers all that morning.

"Then he stopped a minute and said, 'And not a damn one came in.'"

"I won't ever forget his taffy candy," Dry continued. "It was ten inches long, and he wrapped it in white paper, and it'd last you all day long."

More typical Covington wit

Dry's story sounds typical of Covington during his years on the Concord scene. Here's another ad, in which he waxed philosophic:

> *Man's inhumanity to man makes countless thousands mourn. I'm in no frame of mind to preach this morning.*
>
> *Everything has gone wrong this week. A motherly looking woman came in and robbed me while her husband talked to me.*
>
> *Another woman had to tell me that her son was being persecuted; another one that her husband had no chance in life on account of favoritism shown by rich men. Investigating, I find that the son and the husband are not worth a damn. So what?*
>
> *I get to considering my own troubles and want to cry down somebody's neck because I'm sick and nobody cares. I'm broke and the only ones that care are those I owe and can't pay.*

And this is Sunday when everyone is supposed to be at rest and at peace with the world, or perhaps I should say or such as are professional fault-finders, who criticize everything and everybody and make countless thousands mourn those critics. All have their place in the scheme of things; they make the world better with their everlasting fault-finding and criticism. They make people more careful of their conduct and more particular in matters of common honesty and decency, even if they break a few hearts, same as mine is broken.

Won't you come in and cheer me up. I bet I certainly need it. C. Patt Covington.

Pungent thoughts on women

In this one, Covington voiced some pungent thoughts about women.

You can't fool the women. As a small boy I tried my mother, my grandmother, and a few old-maid aunts, and it didn't work at all, and after nearly sixty years' effort I've decided it can't be done, unless, of course, the lady is willing to be fooled. Kipling says, that's another tale.

And there's no bad women. There's foolish women, and wise women, and lazy women, and smart women, fat and slim, large and small, but when one goes bad it's time to holler for a doctor. She's sick mentally, morally and physically, or all three.

Women have three different kinds of influence over men: spiritual, worldly, devilish, and different women offset different men differently.

The spiritual influence of one woman makes a man more reasonable, decent, honest, intelligent, affectionate and charitable.

The devilish influence makes him the opposite of these things.

The worldly influence will make a man buy a car, build a house, take a bath, wash his neck, change his shirts, and like it and never say a word about it.

But all are wise or foolish, none bad. No matter whether they make this life a heaven or hell for the men around them.

Then he put in some advertising, for good measure:

Just in, curry combs, household and camp axes, and hatchet handles, inclusive 12 to 27 inches. Pistol grip, hack saws, and lamp chimneys, wicks and burners.

Come along, come along, let's trade. Auction Saturday, 2 p.m. C. Patt Covington.

An idyllic Mount Pleasant

East Cabarrus County won some of his words of wisdom in the following one.

In gallant old Mount Pleasant, where the skies are very blue,
Where the old maids are the sweetest and the girls are fond and true,
Where the crops of gentlemen are full of heart and sand,
And the matrons and the widows are the finest in the land,
The Barringers and the Mooses are rated mighty high,
And the Heiligs and the Cooks are among the bigger fry, Where the Lentzes and McAllisters are twice as thick as bees,
Around Jim Shith's [Smith's?] garage, that always tries to please....Same at C. Patt Covington's.

Covington, in that same ad, announced he had a shipment of new $5.00 and $7.50 men's suits, lamps, wicks, pencils, "and whit rocks to sharpen anything but your wife's tongue.

Ads filled with bargains, nonsense—and mysteries

After rustling through a scrapbook on Patt Covington and his original pennings, I've found them appealing bits and ditties, sometimes philosophical, sometimes nonsensical. To me, they seem timeless and, in a way, priceless. They're not always happy, but they're always entertaining and revealing.

His advertisements often began with "Come to Covington's Concord, N.C., Concord's original third rate store." One continued: "Book shelf bargains, Testaments 10c each; 3 paper back books, 25c each, regular price, 25c each;

"Free one hatchet or hammer handle with each 25c axe handle...Lock up your house completely, lock sets for dwellings 50c a set complete with screws."

Then Covington quoted from a lady's letter to him, but he never revealed her identity:

> *Dear Pat: You handsome old thing, why don't you come over and see me any more?*
>
> *I want a man like you that will treat me right and rough and oh boy would I work for you honey.*
>
> *I would rather be an old man's darling than a young mans slave, but I won't be your slave and poor darling too—Love and Kisses.*

Was she a widow? An old maid? A marriageable young woman? Was she really after Covington? Or was she just part of his imagination? Whatever the answer, the enthusiastic letter had a dramatic effect on Patt, for he wrote: "My head swelled and busted my headband this week....The doctors at Duke says it will be six months before I can walk, if ever, but they are very enthusiastic about the progress I'm making, but the girls can't see me at all."

I'm not sure whether Mr. Patt was rendered walkless because of the lady's attentions or because of a health problem. Anyway, he then wrote off in yet another direction. "The foot ball scores this fall remind me that a dog can whip a opossum, a opossum can whip a coon, a coon can whip a dog, and that's N.C. Football history for years." Does that have a familiar feeling for anyone?

"Well," he continued, "I have a lot of men's overcoats and all the same size, I'll sell cheap, ditto girls coats also. Lamps, Chimneys, wicks and burners."

Didn't die when he should have

"I'm mighty good. I didn't die when I should. Come on to the wind up and lets trade... C. Patt Covington."

A lot about Cora Lee

Here's an interesting one:

> *Do not have any money, so come quick. You boys might surrender your Cora Lee with this:*
>
> *When the sun sinks in the west, Cora Lee, and I lay one down to rest, love to thee,*
>
> *Every star that studs the sky seems to stop and I wonder why they grow dimmer than your eye, Cora Lee, Cora Lee, marry me; marry me, Cora Lee."*
>
> *But watch for the old man's shotgun and tell her I'll sell her a right nice fur-trimmed coat for $3 and $4;*

> *Honest Injun, and a small book case $5.00; a $15.00 serving table $5; cups, saucers, bowls, dishes and cooking utensils at a good price.*
>
> *So get married and jump for joy!*

The next one mentions Cora Lee again, but I'm not sure what to make of it.

> *Say boy, just think of it. I'll sell you a good coat for $1. Union street stores sell pants for $1, a suit for $2. Come on, lightweight colors, worn and shop-worn both, but a goodbye sale.*
>
> *Did you ever think of what a bunch of go-getters the Concord police force is.*
>
> *Someone stole a fine watch out of the candy shop two weeks ago. We got it back in ten days and the only information we gave them was mis-information.*
>
> *Can you beat it?*
>
> *Cora Lee dishpans 25c, sifters, 15c, perculator* [sic] *tops, 2 for 5c, tire pumps 65c, cast iron skillet and lid $1 each, skillet only 75c, I'm broke.*
>
> *Cora Lee come to me, Come to me Cora Lee. I'm as lonely and distraught as I can be.*
>
> *But the hope that you'll be mine, Gives a solace most devine* [sic], *And that hope I'll never resign, Cora Lee.*
>
> *Marry me Cora Lee, Cora Lee marry me. Not because your face is fair to see, But your soul so pure and sweet, Makes my happiness complete. Makes me falter at your feet, Cora Lee.*
>
> *For sale, five foot show case in good shape, $9; other show cases, 75c up. Grocer scales, weights, 140 lbs to 1,000.*
>
> *Bound to sell. I'm broke.*

His thoughts on movies

Here's one more short ad, a real change of pace:

> *A preacher was talking in here Monday set me to thinking of the right and wrong of picture shows, dancing and dance shows.*
>
> *Now I've seen some rotten shows, pictures and other kinds and some of the best sermons to reach me came in pictures and pictures will gradually become a part of our schooling, no doubt of it.*
>
> *But children and adults will be shown different pictures.*
>
> *This is imperative if we would avoid confusion and juvenile delinquency though it seems to me that the children's morals are as good as their elders, all things considered.*
>
> *Regards to preachers, teachers and P.T.A. members. Suggestion, advice and criticism accepted at value.*
>
> *Hoping to see you all soon if not sooner.*
>
> *C. Patt Covington. Sole prop. of Concord's third rate store.*

1930s merchant's ads offer glimpse of past

Let's take another look at Concord's Patt Covington—town wit, philosopher, candy man and secondhand goods merchant. Here's a good ad:

> *Job complained to his friends, says that women are miserable comforters.*
>
> *That God has delivered himself into the hands of the wicked, that they gape at him with their mouths and wink at him with their eyes, destroy his substance and make a by word of his name, and he curses the day he was born.*

For sale: Big and little bargains

Here's another gem:

> *The thing that worries me most now is making a living, my customers don't seem able to find me down here and I've got a good bunch of bargains too, big tubs, little tubs, buckets and bowls, cups and saucers, dinner sets, both plain and decorated, but if I can't sell I can't eat and I have a pretty good appetite now.*
>
> *Come buy.*
>
> *Job says people who feel secure [are] those whose feet are about to slip.*
>
> *Human nature I reckon though, in fact there are a great many people that have been more than friendly to me, doing too much for me, but I find that Job knew what was what.*

People who take a mean advantage out-number your friends three to one [from] just plain crooks to thoughtless good people like Job's comforters who insisted that he had offended God in some way.

Poor old Job! Poor Pat.

Tin cups, pints and quarters, boot-legger's funnels, tin pie-plates and tin dish pans, blue willow plates, cups and saucers and plenty of candy for the children.

Won't you please help me a little. Now as of Yore. C. PATT COVINGTON.

Preachers and politics

Here's yet another:

Of course I don't know, but it's my opinion that politics have done the church more harm than anything else in the past 40 years.

Preachers began advocating this law and some other law and supporting candidates who were in favor of such and such a law till the burden of their sermon was "pass a law, pass a law."

They first set out to disenfranchise the negro voter, which did no good to the state, but helped the negroes a lot and left the church out quite a bit.

Over in Richmond County where I was born, white suffrage was an issue and the pastor of the leading Presbyterian church was elected sheriff and several preachers to other offices.

Cam Morrison [former governor] started to the Governor's office and the Red Shirts raised hell and scared the senses out of a lot of people who had very little sense to begin with, and I honestly believe if it hadn't been for some of the women taking hold of the situation and helping the superintendent of education build up the school system and churches apart from politics, some people would still be getting white supremacy and singing "Dixie."

However, there may be, there's over a dozen secret, social and political clubs being organized in the country since, not counting the Masons and Odd Fellows, and it's generally true that a man who belongs to the lodge has little time or money for the church.

Come in to see me everybody!

"I look so fine and gay"

Now Patt turns to a kind of fun one:

When I go out to walk about
I look so fine and gay
I have to take a dog along

> *To keep the ladies away.*
>
> *Especially when one's pants leg is rolled up.*
>
> *The idea is to get my leg sunburned to counter irritation—relieves pain, you know.*
>
> *Inasmuch as some good folks have taken offense at me, my silly store and advertising, I apologize and shall endeavor to be more decorous and to be my age—though sixty is not so awfully old.*
>
> *The Cora Lee lyrics are suggestions to young men, as I know of no Cora Lee who can see an old bozo like myself unless he's rich, but I do love a wedding better than any old maid in the world.*

Weddings: "Tickle me plum pink"

Covington sometimes even waxed romantic:

> *It tickles me plum pink to get somebody married and I like to tease girls just as well as any man and if I get a chance I might squeeze them a bit, same as any other man preacher and no harm intended even if I am sixty with a broken leg.*
>
> *Come to me, Cora Lee,*
> *Cora Lee, Cora Lee, come to me;*
> *I am as lonely and as broke as I can be;*
> *But the hope that you'll be mine*
> *Is a solace most divine and that hope*
> *I'll never resign, Cora Lee.*
>
> *Well, I have the usual array of buckets and bowls, pots, lamp chimneys, wicks, burners, coffee pots, cups, fry pans, skillets, bread pans and tea kettles.*
>
> *Well, come buy.*

Olden days not always so quiet

How about a little nostalgia for the olden days of prewar, Depression-gripped, staunch little Concord? In the quiet days before World War II, deep, rumbling, shrieking mill whistles would shake the earth when they went off, first at 6:00 a.m. to awaken mill workers and everybody else. They'd blast again before 7:00 a.m. as a warning to hurry.

Those were the days of the horse-drawn ice wagon, when folks had cards with 10, 25, 50 or 100 printed in a circle on them, signifying the number of pounds of ice a family needed that day. Housewives would hang the cards on their doors. The driver called out, "Ice," and rang the bell on the wagon as the horse plodded along. The driver would chop off the required amount, pick up the block with tongs, sling it on his back and take it to the housewife's icebox. On hot days, kids followed the wagon, stealing ice chips to suck. (I also tagged along, begging the driver to let me ride the horse, which he did.)

Those were the days of walking downtown, holding Mother's hand, for Coca-Cola in a little glass with a slice of lemon at Gibson Drugs, with a lot of other chatting mothers and kids.

On hot nights, it was ecstasy when parents said, "Call Cabarrus Creamery for a pint of chocolate ice cream." A boy on a bicycle would deliver it to your door. (The creamery phone number was 292 and I think the pint of ice cream cost a dime.)

Coal had to be shoveled

On cold days, there were coal furnaces, wood-fired laundry water heaters and open fireplaces, not too many newfangled oil stoves. But—gasp!—one family had a "robot" that automatically shoveled coal into the furnace. (I think it was called Iron Man—a sort of conveyor belt that ran through a rectangular duct from the coal pile to the furnace.) In winter, it didn't take as much ice for the icebox, out there on the screened back porch that joined our kitchen to the house.

Those were the days of three picture shows (movie theaters to you young folks) in downtown Concord—the State, the Pastime and the Paramount. They seemed to stay full most nights. On Saturdays (no Sunday movies, kids), the Paramount featured daylong Mickey Mouse and Popeye Clubs, with cartoons, serials and Westerns from nine in the morning until late in the afternoon. Sometimes admission was six Coca-Cola bottle caps, but fifteen cents did very well—a dime to get in and a nickel for a pound of chewy peanut butter kisses, which lasted nearly all day. You swapped candy with your buddies, of course.

Sometimes the Paramount held talent shows featuring unbelievably tacky costumes and performances. Prizes were movie passes, candy bars and drinks, ten-cent-store jewelry and maybe a dollar or two. Wonderful, we kids thought.

City pool opened in May

In late May, the YMCA's pool would open. I'll never forget the red-and-black Depression bathing suit one youngster wore. When it got wet the first time, the water turned red and black and the suit a ghastly mix.

We always walked to school, and usually home to dinner, too—that is lunch to you younger folks—except on rainy days. Then we yelled with joy when they decided to "teach through" until 1:00 p.m. and dismiss for the day because of the rain. We didn't have school buses in town then. There were no school cafeterias, either. We carried lunch in little boxes or brown bags or walked home for lunch and back.

At Coltrane School, we jumped rope—counting and shouting rhymes—and played softball, kickball, dodgeball and hopscotch like schoolkids everywhere still do. We all participated in big field days each spring, with potato-sack races, human wheelbarrow races, games and sports.

On rainy days we went to the auditorium to learn and sing old Scotch and Irish tunes: "Reuben, Reuben," "Scotland's Burning," "Danny Boy," "Jeanie with the Light Brown Hair," "Flow Gently Sweet Afton" and, of course, "Dixie."

School year got longer

Today's Coltrane-Webb students might hoot at the ornate old brick barn of a school that was home to us eight months a year. (Some recall our outrage when we suddenly had school nine months a year.)

In early years, the schools held graduation exercises for those who finished the seventh grade. That practice stopped, however, because many students seemed to decide one graduation was enough and didn't go on to Concord High.

At Coltrane, when we went up those big gray stone steps and in the door, we were in the auditorium. Mrs. McKay's, Miss Kathleen Smith's and Miss Rosa Caldwell's classrooms opened directly off the auditorium. Sixth-grade classrooms opened off a second-floor gallery that circled the rear of the auditorium. We sixth graders felt grown up, changing classes like the high school kids.

For a long time, the high-ceilinged auditorium had no seats—but that was before my time. Too expensive, in those hard years. During our chapels and programs, we sat on rough, hard upright benches with backs. I've heard those benches were built especially for a tent revival held on Coltrane School grounds in earlier years and then donated to the school. Remembering how uncomfortable they were, I can't say I experienced any particularly religious feelings while sitting on them.

Bell governed the day

The office of stern Principal Webb opened right off the stage at the far end of the auditorium. Beside his door was an ear-splitting brass bell, operated by a pull chain. The resounding clang of that bell governed each day, ringing promptly at 8:20 a.m., and for recess, dinner hour, afternoon and closing. At 8:23 it rang again. If you weren't in your room and in your seat, you were in trouble.

At midmorning recess, we headed, with our pennies, for the basement, where Mr. Williams of Williams Candy Kitchen sold his homemade goodies every day, along with Baby Ruths, Tootsie Rolls and other store-bought candies. No one who ever tasted his homemade taffy—those huge chunks for a nickel—will ever forget that delight.

Fire destroyed old Coltrane School in 1946

Strange how we, as adults, revere those old school buildings that as children seemed like daytime prisons, disciplinary dungeons and dispensers of mounds of homework. A good friend, adept at handwork, rescued several bricks from Coltrane School and years later decorated them with a needlepoint cover bearing our names and "Coltrane School, First Grade, 1931."

A Bonaparte's chandeliers are hanging in Concord

I've run across two short subjects I'd like to discuss: family kin and Napoleon's cousin's chandeliers. On May 8, 1937, four magnificent chandeliers that had hung in the palace of Prince deRohan Bonaparte, a cousin of Napoleon Bonaparte, were consecrated at All Saints' Episcopal Church in Concord. I'd bet not too many people today are left to remember that big day.

Concordian Ada Rogers Gorman, a somewhat eccentric and wealthy world traveler, had bought them, probably the year before, especially to present them to the quaint church that, in 1937, was on Cabarrus Avenue near downtown Concord. To hold those big, beautiful lights, the small church was renovated. The lights were suspended from cross beams below the ceiling. A new furnace was installed as well. Here's how it all came about:

The chandeliers were among seventeen—including a really mammoth one—that hung in the Bonaparte palace in Paris's Latin Quarter. It eventually became the property of France, as the palace was one of that nation's great showplaces. During World War I, the palace was hit by shells from long-range German guns, "much damage being done," reveals a short history of the chandeliers published recently in an All Saints' newsletter.

At war's end, the palace was declared unsafe and was dismantled, and its furnishings were offered at auction. A Mr. Feldman and his five sons traveled to the Paris sale and bought the chandeliers for their three antique shops on the Rue de Royal in New Orleans. The one mammoth chandelier was hung in the Jewish Temple in New Orleans, and the other twelve went to other parts of the United States, "where they are greatly prized" in assembly halls and maybe other churches.

You can see Concord's four today in the new sanctuary of All Saints' parish, which celebrated its 125th anniversary in Concord, and its 30th year at the Concord Lake Road campus, in 1973.

Elegance personified

"Each chandelier holds twenty lights placed artistically amid the tracery of gold leaf, while from concentric circles are suspended prisms that give off a soft tone to the lighting," according to the newsletter article.

"Streaming from the crown above each chandelier are strings of crystal beads."

I'd bet Miss Ada, as she was called, also helped finance the renovations, as she gave the chandeliers in memory of her mother, Martha Rogers.

On May 8, 1937, there was no early service, "because at the 11 o'clock service there will be Holy Communion, as well as the consecration of the new chandeliers and a historical sketch of All Saints' church by the rector. The public is welcome."

Blood ties can be mystery

Now, on to the second topic. The blood ties of family, even to remote cousins over many generations, remain a mystery to me—and probably even to many people who delve into genealogy more than I do. Several years ago, I went to a Morrison family reunion at Rocky River Presbyterian Church. I am descended, through my Caldwells, from pioneers Robert and Sara Morrison, who settled near Rocky River in the 1700s. Among the hundreds reuniting there at the huge covered-dish picnic, I saw a man who looked so much like my father it was startling. He was a bit taller but had the same husky build, brown eyes and ski-jump nose. He was slightly balding—and he wore a clerical collar.

Eventually I said to him, "You look so much like my father it's startling, but he was a Caldwell."

He looked at me peculiarly a moment then said: "My middle name is Caldwell." Of course, I've never forgotten it.

Then quite recently, I went to the ancient Spears Graveyard, near Rocky River Church, where the Daughters of the American Revolution were putting special American Revolutionary War markers on the tombs of my ancestor Robert and his pioneer brother John Morrison. During that event, I struck up a conversation with another attendee, about his T-shirt with a Scottish theme.

We compared families and genealogies briefly, and I ventured that I was a Caldwell before I married. You guessed it. He said: "My middle name is Caldwell." So we find our "cousins" most everywhere these days, especially at family reunions...and that is a good thing.

Mural's unveiling brought folks out in finery

It was a headline event for Cabarrus County, that Friday evening, March 21, 1941, but I'll bet many people, even old-timers, don't know offhand what it was. At that time, newspaper headlines were screaming that Yugoslavia had just signed away her freedom to the Nazis and that the Russians were pledging help for Turkey, should Germany invade. Pearl Harbor and war were nearly nine months away.

But in Concord, the really big story was gentler and kinder, for the enormous wall-to-wall, nearly floor-to-ceiling mural depicting Cabarrus County's history—"said to be the largest of its kind in the South"—was unveiled in a formal ceremony. Perhaps you've seen this work—bold, with Cabarrus people of the county's various periods and locally significant historical events.

Giant mural in community center ballroom

Today the mural stretches over the entire north wall of Cannon Memorial Library's auditorium. But originally, it occupied an entire wall in the ballroom of the Community Center, which formerly stood beside Central United Methodist Church on Union Street North in Concord.

What a night that black-tie, formal-gown event must have been. No less a celebrity than former governor Clyde R. Hoey, in formal evening suit, was guest speaker. The artist, James McLean, who researched Cabarrus history and put it in vivid tableaus on the mural, was there. So were his wife and mother.

The news accounts were lavish in their descriptions of the event, and the local citizens who attended it, in their elegant best. According to an old local newspaper clipping, "In the presence of some 400 local citizens and distinguished guests from all over North Carolina, Cabarrus County's own historical mural, recently painted by James McLean and placed on the West wall of Confederate Memorial hall in the Community Center building, was unveiled Friday evening."

The unveiling honors went to "six young women and six young men, all of them representatives of the families who made the [Cabarrus] history so admirably symbolized by the artist in what is said to be the largest painting of its kind in the South."

Governor speaks at dedication

"Honorable Clyde R. Hoey...widely acclaimed for the beauty and fluency of his oratory, was chief speaker on an elaborate program that preceded the unveiling," continued the report.

With the premise of "Civilization is a covenant between the dead, the living and the yet unborn," Hoey in his flowery old-time way praised everything Cabarrus County. "Scotch-Irish and Dutch pioneers," Hoey said, "who though peace-loving people, were yet ready to sacrifice and even lay down their lives for freedom and justice and other spiritual values they prized."

Hoey touched on the many Cabarrus highlights—the Cabarrus Black Boys, the Reverend Hezekiah Balch and five county men who signed the Mecklenburg Declaration, the people who paved the way to make Cabarrus a separate county, including namesake Stephen Cabarrus. He described George Washington's visit here, noting that the father of our country found Cabarrus County a place with goodly soil.

"Great county"

Hoey noted the two thousand county men who "donned the gray" beginning in 1861 and "defended the cause they believed to be right, the other wars local men and women helped fight."

"You have a great county," Hoey told that august assemblage. "It is a fine thing for you to preserve her history for posterity and to transmit it to your children with all its hallowed memories.

"Life is a high adventure always, and we really have today the same valor and the same devotion to ideals that our forefathers had."

Well-known guests came to the unveiling from all over, another reporter wrote in an accompanying story—the Belks from Charlotte, the Rondthalers of Salem College, the Everetts of Durham, others from all over the state and Virginia. There were locals, too: A.R. Howard, Aubrey Hoover, Jennie Gibson Brown, Agnes Morris, all in the most elegant attire. Mrs. Stahlee Funderburke wore a century-old wedding gown. Anna Walker, Janie Patterson Wagoner and Adelaide Foil appeared in attire of several periods.

There were cheers, the news account reported, as the heavy curtain lifted, revealing the broad panorama. Folks crowded around to see it.

More than pictures on mural

"As they looked, though, it was more than pictures painted on a mural—painted well too—it was their ancestors who made up the fighting Black Boys [portrayed]; it was their two regiments that left for the Civil War," said the article.

> *It was a reproduction of the old court house and more recently it was the remembrance of those who did their part in the last conflict* [World War I].
>
> *Spellbound in awe was the audience when they looked to the figure of Christ on the cross and it was almost with reverence that Concordians saw the history of the past unfold before them.*
>
> *And a treat it was to watch North Carolina's finest come into the hall. . . .*
>
> [Mr. Hoey's wife,] *ever gracious in her charming, lovable manner was handsome in blue sequin trimmed jacket and red skirt.*
>
> [The] *refreshingly democratic Mrs. Charles A. Cannon bustled about with an air of efficiency.*

And of course there was the artist, Jimmie McLean, as he was referred to, who provided a "thorough explanation of the historic background of his mural."

"The success of it all!" the story concluded.

Mural weaves Cabarrus tale through generations

In 1939, the Great Depression was still wreaking its dreary worst on the United States, Cabarrus County and Concord included, but there were good things, too. One of them was the giant mural—fifty-two feet long and twelve feet tall—that depicts major events in Cabarrus County's history and which today, more than half a century later, remains a pristine work of art.

The mural was conceived and begun eighteen months earlier, in 1939. Today, thanks to early research by local historian Elizabeth McEachern Davis of Concord, who was curator of the old center's Memorial Hall museum, where the mural was housed for many years, we have a lot more detail about this enormous work. True, most old-time Cabarrus folk know the mural well, but today, there are many young people and probably thousands of new residents who may not have seen or heard of it. Besides, many of us likely need our mural memories to be refreshed.

Just for starters: The painting's cloth base was woven by Cannon Mills Company, in linen, to the specifications of James McLean.

North Carolina artist McLean joins WPA art program

McLean, Miss Lib Davis wrote, a native North Carolinian, born and raised in Lincoln County, studied art in Philadelphia and Europe. "When the Depression came along, there was little demand for artists, so Mr. McLean joined the W.P.A.," the Works Progress Administration, one of President Franklin Roosevelt's nationwide work projects designed to help speed the nation's financial recovery by employing citizens, including artists. Miss Davis went on:

> *It was through the W.P.A. art program that the mural was painted at a cost to the city of $15,000. Mr. McLean came to Concord in 1939, spending three months studying our county's history.*
>
> *Then with a committee from the county, the* [historic] *highlights* [to be depicted] *were selected.*
>
> *Mr. McLean then went to Raleigh and Chapel Hill, studying these particular incidents at the Archives and the libraries, to be able to portray the incidents correctly.*
>
> *His studio was in Chapel Hill, and that is where the mural was painted.* [In early 1941] *it was brought to Concord on a large Cannon Mill truck and placed on the wall of Memorial Hall."*

Descendants of local history makers at unveiling

At the unveiling, the twelve young people who assisted were all descendants of "those who made the [county's] history"—Emma Lou Lafferty, Jennie Brown, Mrs. Joe Davis Jr., Mrs. Stan Northrup, Rosa Caldwell, Mrs. Stuart Morrison, all of whom wore period attire, and William Flowe, George Richmond Jr., Archie Snyder, Thomas Morrison, Eli Goldston and R. Brown McAllister.

"The mural begins [at far right] with the Indians who lived in what is now Cabarrus County. Only a few [Native Americans] actually lived here, but many passed through." Sections of Union Street were part of the land route known as the Great Indian Trading Path, which crossed the county on its way from South Carolina to Winston-Salem, Davis's account continued. In fact, she wrote, two early paths came together near Cold Water Creek on what is now U.S. 601 south of Concord, "and in that area we find many Indian relics, and again near Kannapolis, as these were camp sites."

Major county history depicted

Next on the mural is the pioneer, "dressed in his 'coonskin cap and leather clothing, [who] is pointing to the future. The first settlers located in the Rocky River section—having come from Pennsylvania by way of the valley of Virginia." Davis then explained:

> *Over the pioneer's head is Fort Dobbs, whose soldiers were responsible for the safety of the people in this section.*
>
> *The original Star Spangled Banner flies over it. Fort Dobbs has been restored and is in Statesville.*
>
> *The three covered wagons with boys with blackened faces are known as the Cabarrus Black Boys' incident.*
>
> [The English king's] *supplies arrived in Charleston and were being sent overland in three covered wagons to the king's soldiers who were in this section of the State collecting taxes from the colonists.*

North Carolinians were rebelling, particularly the Regulators in the Hillsborough area, against paying these taxes, because the money was sent back to England instead of remaining in this state, she wrote. The Black Boys, "who blackened their faces to keep from being recognized, destroyed these supplies" and the irate royal governor ordered them pursued and hanged if caught.

Seven of the Black Boys fled to Georgia after "two of them broke their pledge of secrecy and collected the reward" that had been offered.

Revolutionary, Civil War periods

The county's Revolutionary War period "is depicted with an English soldier on bended knee holding the broken staff of the British flag," symbolizing the break from England and establishment of a new nation—America. "The middle section of the mural is the period of the War Between the States," Davis continued.

"Here we see three companies of soldiers as they left Concord for Raleigh to offer their services to Governor Ellis.

"They had gathered on the lawn of the Court House and heard many prominent men from here and Charlotte speak."

These companies were the Black Boys company, "dressed in black uniforms, under the Confederate Battle Flag; the Cabarrus Guards Company in blue uniforms, and also an infantry company; and the Cabarrus Rangers, a cavalry company depicted by an officer on a white stallion."

"These were the first three organized [Cabarrus] companies to offer their services to North Carolina, it being the day after North Carolina left the Union.

"The families, friends and slaves, dressed in authentic clothing of the period, have come to tell the Boys' goodbye and wish them Godspeed."

Courthouse depicted

Mural artist James McLean and a local committee researched local history and traveled to museums and archives to document the authenticity of the mural's subjects before painting the mural.

The building in the background, according to Miss Lib's research paper listing the events portrayed, is the county's second courthouse, which stood at Union and Corban Streets, where Black's Exxon was located for many years. Fire destroyed this courthouse in 1875. It was replaced in 1876 by the third, or today's "historic" courthouse, at Means Avenue and Union Street.

First gold, county's first cotton mill

"A man panning for gold is next [in the mural]," Davis wrote. And surely most everybody knows the first documented gold discovery in America occurred in Cabarrus County in 1799, triggering America's first official gold rush. "Over the miner's head is a domed building, which is the first cotton mill in the county," she wrote. Dating from around 1839, it was among the first in the southeast. Today it is the imposing Locke Mill Plaza at Buffalo Avenue and Church Street North.

Next the mural covers the Spanish American War in 1898, showing that "The Cabarrus Light Infantry Flag was carried by a company of volunteers from Cabarrus County....The big cannon and steel helmeted soldiers portray World War I." Remember, in the spring of 1941, when the mural was unveiled, the United States had not entered World War II.

"At the end of the mural, we find a man heavily laden with products of the soil; another planting; and crops growing, portraying Cabarrus County's agricultural plenty," Lib Davis wrote.

"With factory steaming, a man holding a cone of yarn and a woman draped in cloth leading to immense bolts of cloth, show the industrialization of the county."

It wasn't too long after it was unveiled on March 23, 1941 that servicemen from all over the United States were looking at the mural.

World War II soldiers see mural here

After America entered the war, military camps were hurriedly thrown up everywhere, including around Concord and Cabarrus County, to strengthen the nation's military power. On weekends, far from home, lonely, with little to do, the servicemen from these new camps invaded the small towns by the thousands, and local citizens often woke up on weekends to find soldiers sleeping on their porches, their lawns or the streets.

Something had to be done. Soon local families were cooking meals for the soldiers—using their few ration stamps—and putting them up on Saturday nights. But their numbers increased. The armory on North Church Street was filled with cots, pillows and blankets every weekend.

But in front of that great mural in the Community Center ballroom, these soldiers were fed, free of charge. This big room was also the Confederate Museum. The center soon became known as the Concord Canteen. Military people jammed into it every weekend, and strictly chaperoned, the men and local girls danced, played cards, played the piano and sang, made friends—and sometimes married—all beneath that room-long mural.

I recall vividly a small soldier who put on the museum's suit of armor and jitterbugged with one of the young belles, the former Miss Alice Craig. There's a photo of that lively dance, with the mural in the background.

Several military companies showed their appreciation of the center's hospitality, presenting the canteen with plaques. They'd also sing to a popular tune, "I Left My Heart at the Concord Canteen."

At war's end, the great room reverted to its quiet fate as a museum.

Center demolished

A lot of memories stayed in that place, and for many it was a sad time when, in the mid-1960s, the Community Center was demolished for a city parking lot. The mural, of course, was saved, although it required unusual care, for in its humongous entirety it had to be transferred from its home wall to a new wall in the new library auditorium, across North Union Street.

"We were worried to death," recalled Branson Jones, who helped in what he thought would be a most delicate removal process. But James McLean, who returned to supervise the move, "literally tore the canvas off the mural's various sections," Jones said.

"He told me not to worry because [he said,] 'If I damage any of it, I'm an artist and I'll just paint it over,'" Jones said.

The move was successful. Today, the mural presides over Cannon Memorial Library's beautiful upstairs auditorium, where meetings, classes, receptions, discussions, music and concerts of all kinds occur. With little trouble, you can see the mural, says head librarian Tom Dillard. Call the library, or come to the front desk during library hours. The auditorium is always locked, but staffers will be happy to take visitors on a brief mural tour.

A last thought: While fifteen thousand dollars doesn't sound like big money today, in 1939, that was a substantial sum. We should thank the WPA and the city of Concord for their artistic foresight.

When old Oscar struck a vein, the government came running

Cigar-smoking Oscar Blackwelder was one of the more unusual characters around Concord years ago, on top of which he produced a rather significant find in a special World War II project.

I remember seeing him drive the city streets in his 1920s-vintage Essex. The car's body was painted bright blue, and its wheels were red. Blackwelder cherished that car. He loved showing it off in Christmas parades and similar events, his cigar smoke billowing along the route.

Mr. Oscar did some unusual things. He had his own gold mine in Cabarrus County. He spent much of his life prospecting for various minerals. He was an expert with dynamite. During the 1930s, Blackwelder worked for New York–based Vanderbilt Laboratories, mainly as a prospector for talc or soapstone, which was used in lubricants, talcum powder, paint, the base for insecticides and hundreds of other things.

That pursuit ultimately led him to a lode of strange, unfamiliar black rock. Our local history treasure Alex Patterson talked with Blackwelder around 1950 and wrote about that conversation. A good thing for us, since Blackwelder has long since passed away.

He found many strange black rocks

Mr. Oscar was a man filled with curiosity. When, while mining, he found a stone he couldn't identify, he'd pack it in an old cigar box and mail it to the

Vanderbilt lab. The lab workers would then send him a postcard with the stone's geologic identification.

In the early 1940s, while Blackwelder was poking around Moore County, near Robbins, he came across a sizable lode of strange-looking solid black rock. He picked up one of the stones and turned it over and over, but he didn't know what it was. So of course he sent it to the lab. But the lab's response to him also was out of the ordinary.

"They didn't send me a postcard," he told Patterson. "They came to see me. A couple of fellows from the lab were waiting for me at the hotel one evening when I came in from the field.

"They showed me that rock," he said, and then they asked him whether he remembered where he found it.

"Yeah," was his typically terse reply.

"Well, let's go see it," they said.

"Nope," he answered.

"Why not?" they asked.

"It's too far to get there before dark. We'll go first thing in the morning."

Feds tell him: Mine it, ship it

At the site the next day, the lab men instructed Blackwelder to "mine it, weigh it and ship it by rail to this address." When he asked them how much they wanted, they replied: "All of it, down to the thickness of a butcher knife blade if the vein tapers that thin."

Now the plot thickens: The lab men then asked whether Blackwelder had a pistol. He said he had a .38-caliber Smith and Wesson back at the house. "Well, you might ought to start carrying it," they told him. Blackwelder said he'd need a permit, and they assured him: "Don't worry. We'll take care of that."

About ten days later, he received a big manila envelope from the Department of the Interior in Washington. "The first thing I noticed," he told Patterson, "was a big gold seal at the bottom of the letter." The letter not only gave him permission to carry the Smith and Wesson, but detailed "what would happen to anybody if they interfered with [his] business."

A few weeks later, the county sheriff stopped by Blackwelder's dig and said he had heard he was carrying the Smith and Wesson. Blackwelder interrupted him. "Sheriff, I believe you are a pretty good fellow and wouldn't want to see you get in any trouble, so, before you go any further, I would advise you to go read that letter up there in the car pocket of my Essex."

He was gone a spell, but when the sheriff came back down the hill, Blackwelder could see he "was two shades whiter."

All the sheriff said was, "Blackwelder, please do me a favor and just forget I was even out here!"

Rock contained uranium

"A few weeks later one of the men from the lab paid another visit," Blackwelder told Patterson, to see how the black rock dig was going and whether there had been any problems.

"No problems," Blackwelder told him, but please, he said, "[tell me] what the heck is this stuff I'm mining."

It's pitchblende, the lab man told him, but that didn't mean anything to Blackwelder, who wanted to know its use. The lab man's reply was noncommittal.

"All he would say was, 'Some people think it can be used to make a powerful explosive.'" It was years before Blackwelder learned that the strange black ore contained uranium. Mr. Oscar had found what was, at that time, the richest vein of uranium ore in the United States.

The ore he was producing had been shipped to Oak Ridge, Tennessee, to make material for the first atomic bomb. I'll have to admit that, while I'd heard some intriguing details about Oscar Blackwelder, I'd never heard that particular account before, so I must thank Alex Patterson.

I don't know what happened to Blackwelder's beloved Essex, although I did hear it had been sold. Even so, what a gripping account to come out of World War II!

War empties dugouts, but Concord lawyer saves local baseball

Concord has been dubbed a historical hotbed of baseball. Nearly six decades ago, however, World War II was taking its toll—and not just on the military and citizens on the home front, but on professional sports, too. Baseball was losing talented players, as more and more able-bodied men, including professional athletes, enlisted or were being drafted into the military.

By 1943, baseball dugouts were rapidly emptying. In 1941, for example, forty-one professional baseball teams were in operation in the area. A year later, there were thirty-one. In 1943, only ten pro teams were playing. Among the baseball casualties that year, reported Hank Utley—who with Scott Verner has published an account of early baseball hereabouts—was the Class D North Carolina State League. That league included Concord's Weavers and teams from Mooresville, Thomasville, Landis, Lexington, Statesville, Salisbury and Hickory.

Utley titled one of his reports "Summer of 1943 in North Carolina: War Time Textile Town Baseball—The Best and the Worst." We'll now take an absorbing look at wartime small-town baseball in this area.

In 1943, baseball down to mill teams, semipros

"It appeared," Utley wrote, "that if these textile towns in piedmont North Carolina were to have any baseball in 1943 it would be semi-pro mill teams playing each other within one town's geographical area."

> *However, one man, C. Manley Llewellyn* [respected lawyer and former judge], *who had been president of the N.C. State league for four years, stepped forth to give guidance and leadership to this historical hotbed of baseball.*
>
> *As president of the now defunct N.C. State league, he encouraged these small textile towns to organize town semi-pro teams that would play close by neighboring towns.*
>
> *Thus was born the Carolina Victory League, semi-pro baseball at its best during wartime restrictions but at its worst with typical textile town intrigue, fighting, gambling and plain ol' baseball cheatin'.*

Forming the league wouldn't be easy, but Llewellyn was up to the task. Llewellyn was a big, muscular man endowed with humor. He was a quick-witted lawyer who settled into his practice after playing briefly for the New York Yankees in the early 1920s.

Mr. Lewlew: I want to see baseball continue

"I want to see baseball continue in the communities of our N.C. State League this season," the man called Lewlew or Mr. Lewlew by many of his friends said in March 1943, "despite the fact that we were forced to close shop.

"It was impossible for our clubs to continue this year due mainly to the player shortage. But that doesn't mean necessarily that baseball in our cities must cease for the duration [of the war]."

People, he continued, "want baseball this year, probably more than ever because a few hours of relaxation and recreation come in handy after a hard day's work." Llewellyn praised Claude Weddington, a Concord team organizer, and Roy Christenbury, a newspaper writer, "for their work on the local baseball front," Utley wrote.

Their work, Llewellyn said, "will mean much to the smaller cities during wartime. It will keep alive the sport for both the players and spectators, and the use of the lights at Webb Field for night games will tend to elevate the game to professional style." In 1943, nighttime baseball games were still quite new—and exciting—to local fans.

New league: Intrigue, fightin', gamblin', cheatin'

In 1943, Llewellyn had "started the ball rolling toward a compact, semi-pro baseball league [made up of aged professional veterans and youngsters] that would give the Piedmont North Carolina home front needed recreation in the midst of ever increasing casualty and death notices from the fighting front," according to Utley. The league also gave a start to a future major league star. Concord native Billy Goodman, who was seventeen when he played in the Carolina Victory League, won the 1950 American League batting title while playing for the Boston Red Sox.

It was to be a memorable summer, with fights, questionable umpiring and other high jinks.

Joining the effort to keep baseball alive was Bill Peeler, a *Salisbury Post* sports editor who added his voice to the swelling enthusiasm for a local baseball league. He wrote: "Thanks to the efforts of Robert 'Red' Ennis [a professional ballplayer who once pitched for the Landis Senators] it looks as though semi-pro baseball will be revived in this section for the duration [of the war]."

He continued, "Ennis has been contacting baseball enthusiasts in several nearby towns" to whip up a wartime league.

Five local towns sign up

Five towns responded with interest—Concord, Kannapolis, Mooresville, Landis and Salisbury. The players would come from the "ranks of Class D professionals and other minor leaguers now working in the local textile plants," plus "up and coming local amateurs," representatives of the towns were told at the organizational meeting on April 2 at a Landis school. (Class D was the lowest level of professional baseball at the time.)

Planners worked toward a schedule of four games per week for each team—two at home and two away. Businessmen who had come to the meeting offered buses to transport players who couldn't use public transportation. It was that very situation that led to naming the league the Gold Highway League. The name referred to U.S. 29, which ran from Salisbury south through Landis, Kannapolis, Concord, Charlotte and Gastonia.

The players weren't going to be paid salaries. Any money they received for their pitching, batting and running would come from gate receipts at the games.

Playing for the fun of it?

It seems, Utley wrote, the players would just be "playing for the fun of it." But there was a serious vein in this planning, as "numerous benefit games" would be played throughout the season to promote the sale of war bonds, Utley wrote. They also would benefit the Red Cross and "in general give the fans a chance for recreation and assistance in the war effort at the same time."

It was a most apropos plan, Utley wrote, stating that the league's purpose was for "recreation and keeping the sport alive while our boys are on the battle fronts."

"They will return some better day after they have made this country and the world a safer and saner place in which to live."

There were wartime restrictions, of course, so league organizers planned to use the uniforms, equipment and ballparks of the Class D North Carolina State League that had suspended operations for the duration of the war. Because most of the players worked at area mills during the day, games would be played at night.

On April 8, the *Tribune*, which had praised the effort, reported the Gold Highway League had been organized. Old-timers from the area will probably recognize some of the names of the league officers and board of directors: Manley Llewellyn was president and Catawba College coach Chubby Kirkland was vice president. The directors consisted of Bobby Hipps, long familiar as a minor league baseball player and manager from Kannapolis; Concord businessman Boyd Horton; George Wright of Landis; Max Brockman of Salisbury and A.S. Jarratt of Charlotte.

Baseball league formed

Said Llewellyn as he accepted the presidency: "The man in the street has spoken. He wants the Gold Highway League." But gas rationing and use of public transportation instead of private cars led to second thoughts on the new league's name. Utley wrote that very few agreed that Gold Highway League reflected the conditions for the wartime rationing, so the name would have to go. "Bill Peeler suggested 'The Worker's League,'" he wrote.

It seems just right that they eventually chose a new name: the Carolina Victory League. The name was officially adopted on April 25, 1943, and referred to "North Carolina and the war victory the entire nation was working and praying for," Utley wrote.

But it was on that same April 25 that the league suffered a blow, a real shocker: baseball-loving Kannapolis dropped out of the league. The reasons were surprising. You'll read more about them later.

Baseball not here in summer of '43

Meantime, all heck was breaking loose for the little semipro Carolina Victory League that summer. Players were getting in fistfights, knife-carrying umpires were being assaulted, big-league scouts were out to steal local players, a few baseball screwballs were keeping crowds in stitches—and Kannapolis was out of the league.

One of the league's aims, declared Llewellyn, had been to give area folks a little recreation, a team to root for, and to take minds off World War II. We were royally entertained, all right.

First of all, Kannapolis, a baseball-loving town, created consternation by deserting the new league on April 25, 1943, Utley wrote. Kannapolis resident Joe Palmisano, who "had a cup of coffee with the Philadelphia Athletics in 1931," released the following statement after the meeting: "Officials in Kannapolis are interested more in winning the war than in baseball." So the league was finalized with Concord, Salisbury, Landis and Highland Park Mills in Charlotte as members.

Comedy added to games

In Salisbury, baseball pro John Heving had lined up some players but no financial backing—until Sam Swartz, a rabid baseball fan, finally agreed to fund the team. Swartz was to play a uniquely comedic role that eventful season.

The Charlotte team had a number of former professionals—probably meaning older players. The official league schedule called for fifty-five games, at four games a week, between May 14 and August 14, and a playoff for the championship. Have some compassion for Llewellyn, who had briefly pitched for the New York Yankees. He "would experience more trials and tribulations in this semipro league than he would in his six years as president of organized baseball's Class D [North Carolina] State League and five years as president of the Class —— Tri-State League," Utley wrote.

It didn't take long for shenanigans to start. In the second game between the Landis Millers and the Concord Weavers, Utley wrote, fans learned "just what a wild and wooly baseball season" awaited them. "In the fourth inning, Landis was winning 5-0 behind the pitching of former Philadelphia Athletics pitcher Herman Fink, a native of Piedmont North Carolina.

"That is when all hell broke loose. Concord scored eight runs on five hits, one walk, three errors and some very questionable umpire decisions."

Fink heatedly questioned a call by umpire Chock Ross of Concord. Then he "backed off and zoomed a baseball" at Ross's head. "His control did not improve," Utley wrote, and "the ball missed Ross' head."

"At that point, Reid Gowan [Landis pitcher, former pro ballplayer and former umpire] charged home plate from the Landis bench." Of course, he headed for Ross, and the two began slugging it out. Other Landis players later said they had a hard time separating the two men.

"George Wright, a Landis team official, said he saw an open knife in Ross' hand.

"Ross, a highly respected semipro umpire, was known to carry a knife in case he needed it for protection.

"Landis won the game 9-8."

There were repercussions, of course. President Llewellyn suspended Fink and Gowan for the season. That action left little Landis with only two quality starting pitchers, Red Ennis and Lefty James. Both later pitched for Concord in the Class D North Carolina State League.

If you found this first baseball brouhaha exciting, the rest of the summer won't disappoint. On June 22, incidentally, the standings read: Landis Millers, 12–9, first place; Highland Park Mills, 12–10, second; Concord Weavers, 11–10, third and the Salisbury Aggies, 7–13, fourth.

Major league scouts steal local players

Professional baseball all over the nation was hurting that summer, from the major and minor leagues to the semipro circuits. "Professional baseball scouts [for major and minor leagues] were beginning to comb the Carolina *Victory League*," wrote Utley. Scouts invaded the Victory League, causing near riots when they tried to sign the local players on the spot—during games, yet.

Here's what Utley wrote about the shenanigans of that spring and summer:

> *Don Harwood, American Legion star from Albemarle and member of the Concord Weavers, was pitching a no-hitter against the Salisbury Aggies, when Claude Dietrich* [scout for the Atlanta Crackers, one step below the major leagues] *called him aside during the fourth inning and tried to persuade him to sign then and there.*
>
> *After* [Harwood] *returned to the mound, Jim Mallory, Salisbury outfielder* [and former UNC star and Washington Senators player and later a Catawba College coach] *homered to start a five-run rally for Salisbury that won the game.*
>
> *Concord's manager, Ginger Watts, was furious over the bloodhound's inopportune tactics.*
>
> *Sam Swartz, general manager of the Salisbury Aggies, also hit the ceiling when Dietrich tried to talk to his players while a game was being played. Swartz called Atlanta reporting the incident, and officials there promised to stop the behavior."*

Ira Thomas, longtime Philadelphia Athletics scout, once invited local player Red Ennis to Philadelphia for a workout with the A's—baseball great Connie Mack's team—but Ennis said no. Ennis later signed with the Boston Red Sox.

Best major league grab: Concord's Billy Goodman

Actually, Utley wrote, Dietrich's prize catch was local baseball great Billy Goodman—seventeen years old that year—who played with the Atlanta Crackers and then signed with the Boston Red Sox and won the American League batting crown in 1950 with a .354 average.

If all that scouting wasn't discouraging enough, some real problems erupted among fans, players and sportswriters over umpiring, Utley wrote. President Llewellyn could hardly keep umpires at the games, what with wartime gas rationing and the umps' irregular working hours. Sometimes umpires simply didn't show up.

A *Salisbury Post* sports reporter wrote:

> *It shouldn't be news to* [Llewellyn] *that fans are more than a little dissatisfied at the handling of the umpire situation and are demanding that something should be done.*

> *For some time now, games at Salisbury have been run by one league umpire, with a player or two from the competing teams filling in where there should be another "blue suit" with eyes.*
>
> *It always makes players serving as umps look bad when they have to call a close play against their own team.*

In fact, one ump hadn't shown up in so long, the article claimed, "you'd think the prexy [president] would realize that he'd quit."

Umpiring continues to be a major complaint

The Dingler brothers, a pair of local umpires, came in for special criticism: "It did not take much imagination on the part of fans to change their name to 'Dingbats.'"

Another, Ed Cross, had a son on the Landis team. He umpired a lot of Landis games. "Of course Ed no doubt was calling 'em like he saw 'em, regardless who was affected, but that didn't keep the bleacher wags from saying Ed had turned over a new leaf and decided to be honest about the whole thing," the article continued.

"But lousy umpiring just irritates the customers so much they can't enjoy the games, and they finally get in the habit of staying at home and reading the papers, where they can get just as mad at John L. Lewis and Hitler without buying a ticket or burning rationed gas," the *Post* item concluded.

"With problems like this," Utley asked, "why would C. Manley Llewellyn love this game?

"It could be that the *Victory League* was doing just what Lew wanted it to do—supplying good family entertainment with a lot of hullabaloo that temporarily diverted their attention away from the war."

Sam Swartz entertained fans, vexed officials

By July 1, 1943, the worst ills of the Carolina Victory Baseball League were ironed out. One of the ridiculed umpiring Dingler brothers—nicknamed Dingbat, of course—had resigned and fled to Akron, Ohio, to call baseball games there. President Llewellyn raised the league's monthly dues from $27.50 to $30.00, and an all-star team was being chosen to play the Navy Pre-Flight School team based in Greensboro. The Navy team featured Boston Red Sox stars Ted Williams and Johnny Pesky, who were then in the military.

In the league that included teams from Concord, Charlotte's Highland Park Mills, Landis and Salisbury, it was the Salisbury Aggies, last in the standings, that was tops at entertaining its fans. Hank Utley quoted a Concord newspaper article describing the antics: "The Aggie general manager, Sam Swartz [who had helped fund the Aggies], was keeping everybody loose with his antics" on and off the diamond.

Sportswriter Fred Severance reported:

When his players ran to the Salisbury dugout to take their first turn at bat, the swarthy Swartz would proceed as though wound up like a mechanical toy in the other direction.

His face reminded us of Charlie Chaplin, with a mustache to match. He would return to the bench with a walk suggestive of Donald Duck.

If he faced a Concord player, his mustache would lift almost imperceptibly, and a word or two of greeting would follow.

The people in the stands loved Sam, according to the article.

As he passed by, one of them would say, "Get in there and pitch, Sam. You can hypnotize the sluggers with your mustache."

We could see that this fellow Sam had scored a bull's eye with the bleacherites. If his flinger [pitcher] *shows signs of falling apart, Sir Samuel, with a shifty glance at the umpire, will enter the sacred precincts of the infield like a dancer leading the grand march.*

A hush descends as the First Citizen of Salisbury approaches his luckless pitcher, gesticulating and waving his arms like Don Quixote's windmill.

He evidently wants to relieve the hapless pitcher in the box, but the southpaw won't surrender the ball and grips it tightly amidst the howls of delight [from the fans].

The one-man comedy is a hit with all except the umpires, who eye the star performer icily from afar.

A "Red Grange push"

Swartz then gave the unfortunate pitcher a "Red Grange push" (referring to the famous football running back).

Sam had definite and far-flung ideas about the boundaries of the strike zone, the article continued. And the umps? When Sam approaches, "They reach for their gas masks as though they had served in World War I."

Dissatisfied, Sam "led the charge—minus his bayonet—to the box seat of Prexy [president] Llewellyn," where they talked for ten minutes, "Llewellyn looking at the sky, Swartz quivering with impatience." Much to Sam's annoyance, the game went on. He gave the umpire and the crowd the "V for victory" sign.

"Fans know that he had just begun to fight."

League plays Navy preflight big leaguers

The Victory League all-stars played Navy Pre-Flight and its big leaguers on July 17, 1943. The big boys, of course, mauled the locals, 11 to 3, Utley wrote. But it's not too discouraging to get beaten by the likes of Williams, Pesky, Harry Craft of the Cincinnati Reds, and Buddy Hassett of the New York Yankees.

But some of the excitement of that big game had evaporated the day before, when "all hell broke loose" at a meeting of Victory League officials. Llewellyn read his statement: "I am suspending Sam Swartz for the remainder of the season on account of conduct and attitude detrimental to baseball." The "detrimental" part was a cardinal sin of baseball—gambling on the outcome of games.

"Swartz immediately appealed. The precarious life of this wartime semipro league was in real danger," Utley wrote. Reaction of the league board was mixed—two supporting Llewellyn, Red Ennis disagreeing. Then Swartz declared he wouldn't let anyone else play on his baseball field. The Aggies players said they wouldn't play for anyone else.

"After this news, Llewellyn stated, 'I don't know just what will happen to the league. I think it would be better for the league to fold than to allow such antics to continue at games.'"

Swartz upset

Comical Sam Swartz was angry over his suspension as general manager of the Salisbury team. "Swartz said he had lost about $1,000 of his own money, but that he had split the winnings with his players" because game-gate receipts were poor and the boys, in effect, were playing just for the fun of it, wrote Utley.

A Charlotte sportswriter blew the betting whistle on old Sam. "I was railroaded," Swartz retorted. Also, Swartz had angered the Catawba College baseball coach over plans to take his college students to try out for Connie Mack's Philadelphia Athletics—and to cancel several league games in order to do it.

The Mooresville Moors, managed by Johnnie Hicks, joined the league late in the summer.

Monster home run

Concord weaver Norman Small, formerly with Mooresville and a minor-league home run hero, hit a gargantuan homer that summer. An area sportswriter reported: "Lost: one baseball. Last seen over the left field fence at Webb Field Thursday night, the destination appeared to be North Union or Church Street. P.S. It was the homer hit by Norman Small." Concord's North Union Street, incidentally, is three blocks from Webb Field, and Church is four.

In fact, Small "literally tore up" league pitchers before he left to join the army in August, Utley wrote.

By late summer, all league teams were scrambling for players. Players were joining the military, or taking summer vacations, or quitting because they couldn't find gas to drive to games. Come August 1, the league all-stars got whupped again by those big-league players in wartime training at Chapel Hill.

League holds Ted Williams hitless

There were a few compensations: the all-star pitchers—Dick Mauney, Virgil "Coddle Creek" Taylor and Red Ennis—held major-league hall of famer Ted Williams hitless in four at bats. That, wrote Utley, "was something to remember."

While the season ended August 14, the fireworks didn't. During the Concord-Landis playoffs, Concord claimed that Landis had used an ineligible player, Roy Pinkston. Pinkston had jumped a contract with Rochester, New York, in the International League. Pinkston argued he didn't know he was ineligible because he was not notified of that fact until August 21. A league inquiry followed. Wrote Utley: "Judge W.G. Bramham, czar of organized professional baseball, replied that Pinkston had not been notified of his ineligibility until Saturday, Aug. 21, so he was eligible to play for Landis until that time." Llewellyn agreed, saying the dates of notification made Pinkston "within his rights signing with Landis."

Landis then accused the Weavers of using two ineligible players: Norman Small and Dub Johnson. Salisbury sportswriter Bill Peeler tried to straighten it all out, Utley wrote. Briefly, Peeler concluded that notification dates cleared Pinkston, and Concord also came out OK, sort of; Concord's two unsigned players, Small and Johnson, who returned to Concord while on furlough from the army, were re-signed by the Weavers before the playoffs. Concord also had used more than the allowed eighteen men per team on several occasions.

Llewellyn threw this jumble to the league's board of directors. Meanwhile, Highland Park (Charlotte) players griped that if an amicable agreement couldn't be reached quickly, they'd stop their season, with no playoff finals.

The league board's vote ruled that both Concord and Landis teams broke the rules, but as Landis won the series, four games to one, the games would stand as played.

Mr. Lew: "He's done OK"

At season's end, Concord sportswriter Roy Christenbury reported: "Lew has had a hard job" from start to finish. "We must say, 'He's done OK.'" In the end, Highland Park won it all on September 2, beating Landis four games to three.

Days later, Utley wrote, "on Sept. 8, the Italian government surrendered to the Allies, but there would be many months of bloody fighting before the world would return to peace." And little mill-town baseball could finally "join the peaceful *National Association of Professional Baseball Leagues*"—the organized minor leagues. What a summer!

Maybe Llewellyn, our 1943 philosopher, got it just right—the Victory League, with all its fights and antics, did what it was meant to: take local Americans' minds off World War II.

Concord general: D-day, medals, aide to presidents

Let's take a look back at a Concord native General Jim Batte, whose accomplishments tend toward the dazzling. In the 1940s, then-Colonel Batte fought in five grim European campaigns and became one of the highest-ranking, most decorated army officers Concord ever produced.

He commanded the Eighty-seventh Battalion, which earned the Presidential Unit Citation for its support during thirty-six hours at Normandy during the D-day invasion. He earned medals galore. He was an aide to Presidents Franklin Roosevelt and Harry Truman. He was promoted to general, right up there with Cabarrus County's General Paul Barringer of the War of 1812 and General Rufus Barringer of the Civil War.

On November 11, 1995, Veterans Day, James Herbert Batte, eighty-two, died at Eisenhower Army Medical Center in Fort Gordon, Georgia.

Batte was, of course, one of hundreds of Cabarrus County's heroes. He went to local schools, graduated cum laude at Davidson College, attended the U.S. Military Academy at West Point and earned his master's in business at Harvard University.

I remember him first from a newspaper interview in August 1945, when I was a college sophomore working as a reporter for the summer. The colonel was home on leave, and my editor at the *Concord Daily Tribune*, Bill Sherrill, wanted a feature story on his combat experiences. Batte looked precisely as a combat officer should—tall, muscular, with black hair and green eyes and erect, as his West Point years had trained him. Here are some of the grim, sometimes funny, homey things he told me that hot, hot August day.

"The first thing I wanted when I landed in New York was a chocolate milkshake or a glass of milk," he said. The first question he popped to his mother, Mrs. George A. Batte of Concord, was how the watermelons and fresh vegetables were doing.

His sharp wit could be self-deprecating. He got the Purple Heart "for not ducking in time," he said, and the Silver Star for "being somewhere [he] wasn't supposed to be." Add to those medals the Bronze Star and oak-leaf cluster.

Saved seventeen from the Holocaust

Batte went into those ghastly German prison camps, including the infamous Buchenwald. At Nordhausen, his battalion saved seventeen men awaiting the crematorium, where two thousand emaciated bodies were found. Also at Nordhausen, he said, starving men were chained to posts, in pits, until they died, when another layer of chained starving men was started, until the pits were filled.

He declared that all the pictures and stories of German atrocities given to the American people could not be exaggerated, that they could not be told in a manner hard enough to describe them fully.

Paris: Ooh-la-la

But Paris, ah, Paris, was different, he told me. It was wonderful, he said—women plying Americans with kisses, champagne, food all along the way and waving flags, shouting, pushing babies to them to be kissed. The best, Batte said, and I remember his grin, "was when the babies were eighteen-year-old blondes."

But he could never get used to "the way even French men would grab American boys and kiss them soundly on both cheeks."

In Paris, men swapped packs of chewing gum for eighty-dollar bottles of perfume, and an odd sight, he said, was the French women in formal evening dresses and high heels bicycling to an engagement.

Germany: "Unparalleled beauty"

Germany, Batte said, was "unparalleled in beauty," especially Worms, where the Eighty-seventh found four hundred thousand bottles of champagne in a warehouse. In Worms they also freed slave laborers in a cigar factory, who promptly handed the American soldiers some "pretty good smokes."

When a radio factory was captured at Halle, every man in the battalion got a Phillips radio. In all, Batte's fighting Eighty-seventh Battalion was engaged in campaigns in Normandy, northern France, the Ardennes, Rhineland and Central Europe.

While Batte was overseas he ran into several Concord boys. Among them were J. Lee Cannon, Bill Lyons, Bill Mills and Frank Day.

After the war, Batte made the military his career, serving with the War Department General Staff in Washington and with Joint Task Force One at Bikini Atoll in the Pacific. He retired in 1970 with thirty-one years of service and earned many other decorations, among them the Distinguished Service Medal, Commendation Ribbon, American Defense Service Medal, American Campaign Medal, Asiatic Pacific Medal, Victory Medal, Armed Forces Expeditionary Medal, Vietnam Service Medal and the Parachute Badge.

Batte is survived by his wife, Elenita Dyer Batte of Aiken, South Carolina, and two sisters, Mrs. K.G. Phillips of Winston-Salem and Mrs. E.L. Foil of Salisbury.

I remember Batte as a thinking, serious young colonel and courtly escort, for we went out together several times over the next year or two. Well, life eventually directed us into different and distant paths, but heavens to Betsy, was Jim Batte ever a good dancer.

Preacher's jog in cemetery discouraged a sin or two

Dare I tell this anecdote, as the preacher told it himself from the pulpit not too long ago? Yes! It's just too good to keep. Besides, a near-overflow crowd at St. John's Lutheran Church heard it during his sermon one Sunday and laughed loud, long and affectionately. For the preacher, some seventeen years before, had been their pastor.

And the episode is Cabarrus County history, of sorts, for it happened maybe twenty years ago, and in this vignette are some delightful glimpses of everyday—or rather, every-night—life in these parts. I just wish I could tell it in the delightfully droll way that Rev. Jack Deal, who was pastor at historic St. John's until 1973, recounted it.

Deal, while shepherding that congregation, was a dedicated runner.

Preacher a dedicated early runner

Now, folks, that was the early 1970s, before running and jogging became the widely accepted nationwide craze it is today. Back then, runners around here were few and far between. They attracted curious stares from ordinary citizens. They were considered peculiar and were eyed with deep suspicion. So you can understand why the preacher was anxious about the reaction, not only from his staid Lutheran flock, but among other residents of those quiet, rural, traditional farm areas in eastern Cabarrus County.

Deal, you see, wasn't certain what they might make of their preacher running aimlessly—to them, anyway—about the countryside, clad in clothing somewhat racy for a clergyman. "I was ashamed for the congregation to see me running," he acknowledged to his former parishioners. "So I ran at night." Late at night—eleven and after.

One moonlit night, coon dog music

Now, late one night, when the moon was full and bright and the weather was crisp and pleasant, the good preacher put on his running attire, white for night visibility, went outside and picked up a trot to start his run. Right away he heard, not too far away, a pack of coon hounds running. Their baying, barking and yelping echoed eerily through the dark. They were apparently in hot and loud pursuit, through forests splashed with silvery moonlight.

(For those unfamiliar with the delights of coon hunting, it should be explained that coon dog owners—like fox hunters—dote on the symphony the hounds create with their baying when they pick up a scent and run the luckless prey through the woods. Fox hunters call that wailing noise "music.")

Anyway, Deal, running to the music of the hounds that night, decided to head down and around St. John's long, ancient cemetery, which lies on a sloping hillside behind the church. He chose the graveyard route, he acknowledged again, partly because it was darker down there and the chance of his being seen by passersby was slim.

Car parked in cemetery

As he trotted briskly along his route, he also noticed, across the cemetery, a car parked near the edge of the cemetery, occupied by a man and a woman, apparently engaged in what courting couples might be engaged in, under a full moon, beside a country church, in an isolated area. Now, if you've never visited the venerable, early American cemetery at St. John's Lutheran Church—perhaps the oldest church in the county, dating from the 1740s—you should. The mortal remains of countless early Cabarrus pioneers, heroes, settlers and others—mostly German in origin—rest in its quiet ground, remote and isolated. It is filled with imposing tombstones and markers. In the oldest section, toward the back near the woods, time and tide have grayed them, worn them, tilted some.

Remember, folks, even the most modern cemeteries can be, well, weird and scary at night, especially when shadows and other strange things seem to shimmer through the moonbeams.

A running ghost?

Picture that pack of baying, running hounds coming closer and closer, and the preacher in his white running clothes jogging his way down, around and back up the other side of the cemetery, through those shadows and moonbeams, and the lateness of the hour.

Well, Deal said, about the time he had wended his way through the tombstones on the other side of the old burial ground, that pack of hounds burst through woods nearby, treed the coon and launched into wild, hysterical caterwauling. At that same instant, the couple in the car heard the wild wailing, raised up, then apparently spotted a figure clad in white moving through the tombstones, looking like something out of this world in that silvery moonlight. A gasping moment or two later, that automobile screamed to life, scratched off and screeched away, motor revving like crazy.

"Those car wheels," the preacher said solemnly, as the congregation shouted with laughter, "dug six-inch-deep trenches" at the edge of the cemetery.

1978: The soggiest Christmas parade ever

I recall a certain Concord Christmas parade day, back in 1978, when the weather was lousy, and it makes me chuckle to this day. It was a wintry Wednesday, November 29, when that unusual Christmas parade wended its way from Cabarrus Memorial Hospital to the courthouse downtown. Here's how the Thursday, November 30, 1978 edition of the *Observer* reported the parade:

> *CONCORD—Promptly at 4 p.m. Wednesday, just as Concord's 50th annual—and longest-ever—Christmas parade was heading out, the icy, day-long rain turned into a wind-blown deluge, scattering the few spectators and drenching the colorful floats.*
>
> *That was the good news. From there on, it was all downhill.*
>
> *Not only were there no fair skies, marching bands, horses or clowns, or even people on the carefully decorated Christmas floats.*
>
> *There was no Santa Claus.*
>
> *While his big rented, but empty float glided grandly down the parade route, Santa was pacing up and down in the boiler room at Cabarrus Memorial Hospital, waiting for his driver to pick him up.*
>
> *"To say I was uncomfortable about the whole thing would be an understatement," said Santa, Norm Stevenson, 33, of Concord, a restaurant supervisor.*
>
> *It wasn't just because he was sweating out the wait and getting hot under the collar because the professional float driver never showed.*

"I had on thermal underwear and all that suit, and that boiler room was hot," Stevenson explained Friday. "I did a lot of pacing.

"I told myself surely they won't have the parade without Santa.

"Finally, at 5 o'clock, I called the chamber of commerce and asked the girl if there was a Christmas parade. She said yes, it was passing right now.

"Then I asked her if there was a Santa Claus float in it, and she said yes, it had just passed and there wasn't any Santa on it."

Santa float driver got lost

The article continued:

> *The Santa float driver, who had gotten lost trying to find the hospital, had found the parade.*
>
> *Santa or no Santa, the driver broke right into the procession about a third of the way through the line.*
>
> *The parade had split into segments, and after the Santaless float sailed through the downtown, many of the several thousand determined watchers, braving the weather under awnings or in cars, thought it was over and began leaving.*
>
> *The float judges went inside. Cars began pulling in behind the Santaless float.*
>
> *But here came the last two-thirds of the parade.*
>
> *The judges put their raincoats back on and came out again. Traffic halted and snarled.*
>
> *Bewildered spectators came back and watched as more peopleless floats glided silently by.*
>
> *The only two marching units that participated despite the weather—the Fairfield Drill Team from Charlotte and the Central Cabarrus High School Drill Team—marched soppingly but snappily by.*
>
> *Afterward, no one wanted to be quoted, because everyone, while deploring the day's events, couldn't talk about them without laughing.*
>
> *"But I just wanted to cry when that float went by without Santa," said one mother. "It was so pitiful."*
>
> *The parade chairman, Concord Alderman Johnny Howard, has gone out of town. There's no indication Wednesday's events led to that decision.*
>
> *Kent Prewitt, Concord Chamber of Commerce director, who has worked with Christmas parades for 17 years, said dryly that the day could be called "somewhat of a disaster."*
>
> *And Santa? He said he'll be back next year, "if they'll ask me."*

Today, I don't recall what weather forecasters had predicted for that parade day. But apparently it wouldn't have mattered, even if the prognosticators had declared "rain," or even "icy, heavy rain." The Christmas parade had to go on.

Those rollicking old-time politics

It's time to take a look back on gentler, if still political, times in Concord, a few years before the Civil War began. Let's start with what today would be a real headliner: "The Cotton Factory in this town was sold on Thursday last, bringing $16,500. John McDonald, Esq., former Superintendent, was the purchaser. The establishment originally cost upward of $40,000."

And that was it. The whole story, in the *Concord Weekly Gazette* of 1857. Today, such a sale would produce long news columns, features, pictures, interviews of all sides—and on and on.

Concord's first cotton mill sold

Concord's steam cotton mill, built in 1839, became the McDonald mill years after the Civil War, then Odell Manufacturing Company, then Locke Mill, among others. McDonald, a transplanted Yankee, ran it successfully through the four war years, selling its materials to the Confederacy. Today, of course, it's Locke Mill Plaza, a condominium/office/restaurant complex, up there at the top of Union Street North.

These neat bits of history come from abstracts of the *Concord Gazette*, published in book form by Kannapolis historian Judge Clarence Horton and Kathryn Bridges, now retired from Cannon Library's Lore History Room.

The sale of the mill must have been a private transaction, as it was not advertised in the *Gazette*.

Lots of news, mostly political

There was much news in that small paper. Unfortunately only a few copies survive, beginning in March 1854 and ending in 1857. So let's savor them.

Concord was a growing little town, but still a quiet one, in 1856, and of course national elections, as usual, ranked high in interest among local folk. On March 27, 1856—nearly 150 years ago now—the *Gazette* reported: "A large number of the citizens of Cabarrus met in the Courthouse" to ratify the Philadelphia convention's nominations of Millard Fillmore for president and Andrew Jackson Donelson for vice president. Benton Burns chaired the local meeting, and James M. Henderson (the *Gazette*'s editor) was appointed secretary. Then W.S. Harris "explained the object of the meeting in a few forcible and eloquent remarks." Victor Barringer also spoke, along with his brother Rufus, who later became a Confederate general.

The chairman appointed committees "to attend the two Nominating Conventions." The group then "resolved that the proceedings of this meeting be published in our town paper, and that other papers friendly to the cause be requested to copy." Oddly, nowhere in the article was it mentioned which political party was holding the convention in question.

A bit more about Fillmore

In 1856, Fillmore had been nominated by both the American Party (also known as the Know-Nothing Party) and the mostly southern remnant of the disintegrated Whig Party, on whose ticket Fillmore had been elected vice president in 1848. He succeeded fellow Whig Zachary Taylor as president upon Taylor's death.

According to the *Grolier Multimedia Encyclopedia*, "the American Party was an anti-foreign, anti-Roman Catholic political organization that flourished between 1852 and 1856 in response to massive immigration." Many immigrants had become part of urban Democratic political machines, much to the resentment of non-Democratic old-stock Americans. "In the early 1850s, various anti-immigrant organizations joined to form the new political American Party—also known as the Know-Nothing Party because members answered 'I know nothing' about the exclusive, native-Protestant organization."

Locals approve state, national ticket

Now we fast-forward to May 17, 1856, and we learn that another political meeting of our local group, on May 10, produced several presidential resolutions:

> *We highly approve* [the nominations of Fillmore and Donelson] *and we will give our hearty support in securing their election, as the only means, in*

our belief, of preserving the union of our glorious Republic and giving a death blow to fanaticism.

That the nomination of that noble patriot, John A. Gilmer, will receive our hearty support for Governor of North Carolina.

That we will use every honorable means in our power to carry out the American Principles: as adopted by the recent National Council.

That it is expedient—to a unified effort of the American Party—to hold a Convention in the town of Concord, say Tuesday of our Superior Court, to nominate candidates for the Senate and Commons of next General Assembly of North Carolina.

In *Gazette*'s waning days, an ill wind brought snow

In January 1857, despite a prominent doctor being found frozen to death, record snow, elections and other local happenings, the newsy *Concord Weekly Gazette* was wobbling on its last legs. What a pity the small weekly, delivered every Saturday, had to end, for it is among the few small remaining windows opening directly into the mid-nineteenth-century past of this area, with its folksy bits, its court, humor and everyday life coverage, its tax and political items, its marriages and deaths.

With the end in sight, the *Gazette* still abounded with fascinating bits of news. First, the blizzard.

"From every quarter come particulars of the recent snow and wind storm," the *Gazette* reported. "It was remarkably severe in this region, the snow lying to the depth of from eight inches to three feet."

A tragedy of that snowfall came with the finding of the body of Dr. Charles W. Harris, former longtime citizen and prominent physician, "now of Newton."

"We are pained to learn that [Dr. Harris] was found on the morning of the 20th instant, a few miles above this place [probably Concord], frozen to death.

"It appears from the evidence elicited before the Coroner's jury, that he had left the home of Mr. James Irvin, the night before, at a late hour, to go to Mr. Bradford's, and it is supposed that on the way thither he either left his horse or was thrown, and endeavored to find the way across the field on foot, where he fell into a branch and got thoroughly wet—from the effects of which he became almost instantly frozen, as he was found but a short distance from the branch."

The coroner's verdict: "Death from Exposure." The good doctor "leaves a large circle of friends and acquaintances to mourn his sad end."

Deep snows problematic

The deep snows brought this area to a standstill; in fact, it kept trains from running. "We were so unfortunate as to be away from home at this time, and in consequence of this, as well as one of our main hands taking advantage of our absence to 'absquatulate' [head for the hills], no paper was issued" last week, editor James Henderson wrote. Henderson apologized, and hoped "our patrons will not judge too harshly of our shortcomings," especially the "paying patrons," but "to those blood-suckers who never pay we say—we don't 'care a red' if they ever get another newspaper."

On February 7, 1857, Daniel M. Fink advertised his studio "where Ambrotype likenesses were available." Also, the "Messrs. Pinkney" opened operations in Concord as engineers and machinists, and the paper said "we wish them success"—especially since they advertised in the *Gazette*.

The weather still raged. The paper said, "[It] has not abated much in severity; in fact, rain, sleet and snow seemed to be the order of the initiatory month of 1857, and we are glad it is gone, though February, as yet gives little promise of change for the better.

"We noticed but one sleigh out here during the recent snow, but it improved the occasion, its jingling bells were heard till even a late hour of the night."

There was a postscript: "The 3rd, 4th, and 5th inst. here have all been beautiful spring weather days—and we hope 'Winter's icy reign is o'er.'"

The next four issues of the *Gazette* listed mainly weddings and deaths. But on March 7, Henderson wrote: "We learn from the Agent at our dept, that there has been shipped from the point on the N.C.R.R. during the last 20 days fifteen hundred barrels of flour and four hundred bales of cotton—If any other station on the line can come up to these figures, we should like to hear of it." How did those cotton bales get there during the earliest beginnings of spring? The *Gazette* didn't say.

After a few choice words, *Concord Gazette* expires

"We never shun a Grave yard—on the contrary, it is about the first place we visit in a strange town." Well, Henderson chose an odd topic to go in the final edition of his *Gazette* on March 7, 1857. I'm afraid Presbyterians today may find bits of this look back, well, uncomfortable.

After his elegiac and a tad critical thoughts on cemeteries, Henderson then announced the demise of the *Gazette*, explaining it to be "The result of a proposition we have received to remove to a new field of labor, which holds out to us the promise of more success and pecuniary reward than we have realized." But he didn't say what that new field of endeavor was.

But back to the graveyard. "The solemnity which it inspires is grateful, rather than disagreeable," Henderson wrote of the burying ground.

"It has no superstitious terrors for us. We love, when the sun is slowly sinking to rest, to wander among the tombstones," some of which are "covered with the mosses of three score years and ten and others of more modern date.

"We love to read the inscriptions—the recorded virtues of those who sleep beneath and await the trump of the resurrection morn—and ramble thro' the paths worn by the slow feet of sorrow and sympathy as it followed love and friendship to the Grave."

Three score and ten is seventy years, and in 1857 that would have taken those tombstones back to the 1780s. In 1857 Concord, he continued, there were only the Presbyterian and Lutheran cemeteries, and the Lutheran "tolerably well kept—the wall not being positively down to the ground and there being some show of respect by the friends of the Dec'd, for their last resting place."

Presbyterians, no respect?

"But the former—the Presbyterian Grave Yard—'is a monument of shame' to those interested in it," Henderson wrote.

> *The wall is down in many places, stock run at large upon it, and in short it is in a very bad condition.*
>
> *Do the friends and relatives of those who lie there neglected ever visit the spot? In charity we should say not.*
>
> *Surely they have more respect for the graves of their fathers, than to let them lie there as they do, their bones almost bleaching in the storm. Cannot something be done to remedy this state of affairs?*
>
> *Among the many calls upon the public purse made from the sacred desk and privately, can we not raise a small fund for the repair of our future dwelling place?*
>
> *We think we might. If not, then let us suffer the tribes of unexplored Africa and undiscovered somewhere else to rest for a short time while we contribute our mites to the formation of a fund for the improvement of our Grave Yard.*
>
> *What say our friends the Pastor and members of the Presbyterian Church whose fathers, mothers, brothers, sisters and children "sleep the sleep that knows no waking" in that neglected, downtrodden Grave Yard!*

The First Presbyterian Church had already built a new place of worship away from that old graveyard, today the uncommonly beautiful Memorial Garden on Spring Street South. Did they perhaps forget their old burying ground?

There were a few more news odds and ends before Henderson wrote his grand finale—a few births, a few deaths and then a real shocker, as a matter of fact. For J. McDonald "stated he had bought the Concord Factory, and could fill orders for yarn, rope, sacks etc."

Now, the local politics of that day do seem odd.

Some local politics

Through a local "Vox Populi," Rufus Barringer was running for town intendant, and "Jas. C. Cannon, A.J. Yorke, John O. Wallace and L.S. Bingham" were seeking to be town commissioners. Their opposition, sponsored by simply "many voters," included R.C. Cooke for intendant and Matthew Goodson, S.G. Murr and J.N. Brown for commissioners.

The winners? Intendant Barringer and Commissioners Cannon, Brown, Goodson and John J. Patterson, who may have been a write-in candidate. (You remember Rufus Barringer, who rose to Civil War general.)

Well, Henderson then said good-bye.

And now, good-bye

"We regret our interests demand that we should thus sever, in some measure, the ties that bind us to Concord, and to many of our patrons, whose generous support—and uniform kindness towards us, will ever be gratefully remembered," Henderson said.

> *Though we confess our expectations, with regard to the success of a press here, have come much short of realization, we cannot but think that as intelligent and reading a people as those in Cabarrus, ought to support one in their midst.*
>
> *And we believe [even with the difficulties encountered] the want of a city newspaper will be felt.*
>
> *We hope before a great while, some one else, if not ourself, will establish another newspaper in Concord, and that our people will encourage it, liberally, instead of sending their money to the North for such papers as the* Saturday Evening Post, New York Herald, *and* Tribune.

He thanked his paying customers, told the unpaid "we need the money and it will be thankfully received."

But what shall we say to those who have never paid, and never expect to pay?

We give them up to the gnawings of a guilty conscience, if so be they have any conscience at all.

In conclusion, we remark that those [who] *have overpaid for the* Gazette, *will be furnished with some other State paper in its place.*

And sadly, the final word came from Horton and Bridges, who wrote in their edited collection of *Gazette* articles: "No further issues of the *Gazette* were published." Sigh!

Oddly, Concord has more than one city incorporation date

It seems really strange that on December 7, 1937, Concord was having a swinging one-hundredth anniversary celebration. Governor Clyde Hoey came to orate, and "friends and neighbors from miles around" descended on the town.

The new armory was dedicated. There was a grand ball, choral singing, a tea for the ladies and field drills by Woodmen of the World. And amazingly, after Concord's big parade, its mobile units drove to Kannapolis "so that Towel Citians unable to attend the celebration [could] view the procession."

One hundred years of prosperity, wars, joy and sorrow

It must have been a really big day, to observe Concord's "one hundred years of growth, prosperity, wars, joy, sorrow, depressions, bad times and glad times." Now, just how is that? Concord's town limits were laid out in 1796, right? That's more than two hundred years ago and four long years after the North Carolina General Assembly, in 1792, established the new county of Cabarrus—and a good deal more than one hundred years before that 1937 celebration.

Well, it seems that the city's one-hundredth celebration that year related to its official incorporation, by which the state allowed it to have a city government, according to a December 7, 1937 article in the long-defunct Concord *Daily Herald Observer*. Frankly, this is confusing to me, after considering the several times in our history that Concord's aldermen sent various documents to Raleigh for incorporation purposes. (More about this later.)

Anyway, the article claims the day was to honor the "100th year under a city government." Whatever. Let's get back to the fun part.

Parade of Progress

That grand day featured the Parade of Progress, with "ten beautiful floats," prizes and judging by dignitaries from Raleigh, Charlotte and Gastonia. Parade master was W.G. Hunt. The parade left at nine in the morning, near St. James Lutheran Church on Union Street South, led by a float carrying Miss Adelaide Blackwelder, "recently chosen as Queen of Concord." The procession went up Union Street North to Locke Mill, turned right on Buffalo Avenue, then right on Church Street and disbanded at Corban Avenue.

Spectators saw decorated floats in several categories: the best historical float, the best commercial float and so on. There were more, entered by private concerns. "Everyone is invited and it looks as though everyone is going to attend," the article claimed. And all that's just for starters, folks.

Four bands performed—the Kannapolis Band, the Franklin Mill Band, the Albemarle Drum and Bugle Corps and the North Carolina A&T College Band. Introductions were elegant at the 1:00 p.m. dedication of the then-new armory. Hoey was the "spotlight of the afternoon," with his dedication address. George W. Coan Jr., the state's WPA administrator, formally presented the armory to the city. Captain C.N. Alston accepted the armory on behalf of the city, and Brigadier General J. Van B. Metts accepted it on behalf of the North Carolina National Guard.

Concluding the ceremony was "a program of Negro spirituals by a picked group of [African American] singers."

Everybody honored

At noon, the Concord Rotary Club hosted Hoey and others. That evening, Concord firefighters similarly entertained them at their annual banquet at the Hotel Concord. The afternoon tea entertained visiting ladies. What a memorable day in the city's history! And would you believe, the concluding Grand Ball that night was free to everybody.

It does seem that the old *Herald Observer* was right: All of these good times and bad times had "combined to make Concord the great little city that it is."

Concord's beginnings

Here comes more about the origin of our county seat. Remember, 1937's city fathers apparently ignored the 1796 doings when city limits were stepped off, in the then-wilderness here. Well, some generous soul left me a goodly pile of papers telling us a lot more about those eventful days. Many thanks to the donor.

One source was an article written by Ed Kestler, a local printer, newspaper editor and one-time postmaster with a little political experience. His long article appeared in the *Concord Daily Tribune* on December 8, 1937, a day after that big one-hundredth anniversary celebration. Another source was R.W. "Wash" Allison, an odd, wealthy, lively character with a mind like a steel trap well into his eighties. He remembered and wrote much of our history in the 1890s. So we'll look at what those two have to say about Concord, although Mr. Wash dealt mainly with the formation of Cabarrus County, always a fascinating topic.

Ed Kestler wasted no time getting down to business in his article. First, he published a letter from Stephen Cabarrus, the esteemed Frenchman and speaker of the North Carolina House, to Cabarrus residents after the legislator gave us our new county in 1792. Written in Fayetteville on January 7, 1794, it reads:

> *Gentlemen, Permit me to convey to you, through the medium of your standing committee, the sentiment that I shall ever entertain for the high honor I have received from the General Assembly of the state in naming your respectable county after me.*
>
> *Such an honor I did not expect, and so greatly I value it that every step in my future career shall continuously be directed to preserve it unvitiated. I am about returning to private life, but be assured that I am well spared that that alone will give your county that dignity to which it is so well entitled.*
>
> *With the greatest respect and affection, I am, gentlemen, yours, etc., S. Cabarrus.*

You may know that Cabarrus people didn't act quickly to decide on a site for their new county seat; it took them four years, to the embarrassment of local leaders. Wrote Kestler, "When the occasion arose in 1796 to name and form a town, citizens south and north and west and east of the present site fought to have it located as each faction wanted it."

Call it Concord for peace

According to Kestler's article, "To settle the division of sentiment, all agreed to leave the location to Mr. Cabarrus," who considered all interests and then named a site in the center of all the contentions, which is the present site, and he said let it be called Concord for peace. "Thus it got its name. The General Assembly passed an act in November 1795 legalizing the forming of a town."

Most old-timers here know that is just one version as to how Concord came about, but note that all these doings were in 1795 and 1796, when the limits were walked off, beginning at a stone, still at the intersection of Union Street South and Cabarrus Avenue. Incorporation came in 1837.

I guess the exact process is lost to us. One version has the state legislature reprimanding us for being so slow-footed—and Stephen Cabarrus did write us another letter, suggesting we forget our individual interests and name a site. In his article, Kestler included the indenture made on February 4, 1796, between the county and John Means, James Scott and Leonard Barbrick, as public commissioners, "to superintend the public buildings."

The document then ordered that they pay Samuel Huie 25 pounds (then about $125), for a tract of twenty-six acres, "lying and being on the waters of the Three Mile Branch, near said Samuel Huie's land and plantation where on he now lives, for the express purpose of erecting the public buildings" of the new Concord.

Excitement reigned at 1796 Concord land auction

Some accounts of the founding of Concord say our pioneers' excitement ran high on the day in April 1796 when lots on twenty-six acres of wooded land were to be auctioned off. That local event today is described in historical markers, smack-dab in the middle of downtown Concord.

In 1796, just twenty years after the signing of the Declaration of Independence, folks hiked, rode horseback or bounced to the scene in wagons from Rocky River, St. Johns and Poplar Tent and other sparsely settled communities then, agog with anticipation. People came in droves, several early accounts claim. They brought picnic lunches with them and prepared for a memorable day to help give birth to the city of Concord.

Kestler wrote that things were arranged by the new town commissioners, Means, Scott and Barbrick, who laid out the new lots. He recorded the names of the people who bought the land, and you'll still find many of their descendants in Concord and Cabarrus County today.

Those very first buyers

"Samuel Hill bought the first lot for 10 pounds, Heath McCachern bought the second for 7 pounds, 15 shillings," and commissioner John Means bought the next, Kestler wrote. Others bidding successfully for those first lots, he wrote, were John Barringer, Leonard Barbrick, James Scott, John Harrington, William Atkinson, Henry Plott, George Carter, Francis Ross, Thomas Maxwell, John Simianer, John Tavenor, Aston Cauble, Wallace Spears, Michael Winecoff, Richard Fouable, William McKnight, Stephen Hadley, Silas Shinn, Henry Furrer, Phillip Kress, Fred Miller and Sam Ferguson.

Also, George Harris, Ryenkold Abenshine, George Masters, Robert Smith, Ben Shinn, Martin Hargey, John Shaver, Hugh Rogers, Jacob Lewis, David Carlock, Charles Hanes, Joseph Bradley, Matthew Hary, Leonard Lyerly, Dan Little, John Rhinehardt, Will Belk, John Hoose (Moose?), William Scott, John Tyler, Robert Hope, Sam Wilson, David Purviance, Robert McMurry—and, Kestler added, "etc."

New village assumes duties

The new landowners paid up to ten pounds per lot and were given deeds that same year. Then came the village's new duties, although Kestler's account seems to skip about a bit. In those days, Kestler wrote, "The town was run by acts of the General Assembly, the town commissioners levying taxes and working the streets, etc., as per said acts until the General Assembly of 1850–1851, when it was formally organized into a town proper.

"There were four commissioners elected and an intendent [*sic*] of police, who ran the town until incorporated.

"By act of the legislature of 1874, the first mayor was elected, John J. Cross."

There was even a commission of health, with "Drs. Gibson, Fox, Orr and McAoe," our historian wrote.

Now, don't ask me why there were so many different town incorporations, starting with the one in 1837, whose centennial Concord enthusiastically celebrated in December 1937.

Finding incorporation answers nigh impossible

Finding those answers would mean going through many old town and state records—and I haven't found any Cabarrus lawyers or town officials today who can explain it. Anyway, by 1852 Concord had four police officers. They were required to patrol the town two nights each week. In 1857, "the town passed a law fining any white person $25 who gave to any slave [except his own] any liquor."

That same year, Rufus Barringer (later a Confederate general), was intendant of police, and James C. Cannon, James N. Brown and John Patterson were his commissioners. Ed Kestler listed almost everybody: the police "intendents," town commissioners and town committees through two hundred–plus years, which I won't burden you with today. Back then, the commissioners were local men, forefathers of many city residents today.

Who were Concord's mayors? The first elected mayor, John J. Cross, was elected in 1874. There may have been mayors before Cross, but they may have been appointed; I'm not sure.

The mayors and other officials

Since Cross, serving terms of from one to four years, these were Concord's mayors until 1937: Charles O. Montgomery, 1876; James N. Brown, 1877; W.G. Means, 1880; R.S. Harris, 1882; J.T. Fisher (resigned), 1883; W.J. Hill, 1883; W.G. Means, 1884; J.L. Boger, 1888; W.G. Means, 1891; Charles McDonald, 1893; J.L. Crowell, 1894; L.M. Morrison, 1895; George W. Means, 1898; M.B. Stickley, 1901; John Brice Caldwell, 1903; C.B. Wagoner, 1909; A.F. Hartsell, 1913; C.A. Isenhour, 1916; J.B. Womble, 1921; C.H. Barrier, 1925; W.A. Wilkinson, 1930; W.A. Wilkinson, 1937.

Kestler also listed the recorders, who were judges of a minor court: Ross McConnell, H.S. Puryear, A.H. Palmer, Daniel Furr, M.H. Caldwell, C.M. Llewellyn and Zeb Morris Jr.

Chiefs of police were J.L. Boger, Marshal Mabery, C.A. Robinson, L.A. Talbirt and H.F. Widenhouse. Postmasters were J.O. Wallace, Mary Dusenberry, J.B. Sherrill, G.L.

Patterson, M.L. Buchanan, John L. Miller, W.B. Ward, J.F. Harris (acting), Ed Kestler and B.E. Harris. Apparently, the first woman to hold public office was Dusenberry. And Kestler, you note, was a postmaster.

Frustration: Concord's incorporation process is never actually defined or explained. Kestler said the city "was first incorporated in 1950–51" (surely a typo, which should be 1850–51), but other sources list other dates.

Anyway, the governing body's official name was Commissioners for the Town of Concord. "In 1903 the legislature changed the official name to the 'City of Concord.'"

Not all was perfect

One of these days I might be able to sort these dates out, but I'm not hopeful.

There were negatives under that first charter, Kestler wrote, because voters couldn't vote for the town commissioners unless they were "white and had $500 worth of property for taxes." Thus, Johias L. Bunby, W.M. Freer, Alfred Brown, Daniel Wagoner and Rensom Winecoff were elected as the first town commissioners. In 1877, the mayor was accorded status as a justice of the peace and allowed to try cases.

In 1887, a cotton weigher was allowed to collect ten cents on each bale sold in Concord. And in 1889, the town was divided into four wards.

Graded school, water and power established

A year later, in 1888, "The city first established graded schools" through an election. The year 1901 was another significant year, as the town was given permission to establish a board of water commissioners. They were M.H. Caldwell, M.L. Brown, W.R. Odell and J.W. Cannon.

In 1905, a power department was added—today's Light and Water Department. In 1907, the cemetery board was appointed. Soon, franchises were granted to Southern Power and Piedmont Carolina Railway Company.

Kestler also did a little blowing of the town horn. Concord, he wrote, had a good city library and "an elegant armory"; the power and light company was free of debt, and Duke Power Company lines furnished power to manufacturers. Furthermore, Concord was a "broad and liberal city" with "all social activities" and growing in values. It also was the county seat of "one of the most prosperous counties" in the state.

"She" had a hundred-thousand-dollar post office and a ten-thousand-dollar city hall. Jitney services, railroads and truck lines "give splendid services," he wrote.

Well, now, how's all that for a quick summation of our town history?

Index

C

D

E

F

G

H

I

J

K

L

T

U

V

W

Y